"Wish You Were Here"
Vintage Postcards of Norwood, Massachusetts

PATRICIA J. FANNING

Published by Rock Street Press
www.RockStreetPress.com

ISBN: 979-8-9894162-0-2

CONTENTS

ACKNOWLEDGMENTS

Quite frankly, this volume would not have happened without Robert Donahue and his daughter, Susan. Bob has been gathering Norwood memorabilia for decades. He has amassed a remarkable and diverse collection, first with his business partner and friend, Bob Hansen, and later, assisted by his daughter, Susan Donahue. Susan has utilized her own artistic skills to organize, catalogue, and display the multitude of photographs, artifacts, and documents that they have assembled.

Postcards from the Robert N. and Susan Donahue Collection make up the entirety of this work. I cannot thank them enough for sharing their collection, knowledge, and enthusiasm for all things relating to Norwood. These images capture the history of this Massachusetts town from a unique perspective; I had only to add context and captions.

INTRODUCTION

Norwood was originally a village within the town of Dedham. Some fourteen other communities throughout eastern Massachusetts – from Wellesley and Natick to Bellingham, Wrentham, Plainville, Walpole and on and on – were part of the huge land grant awarded by the General Court in 1636 to the proprietors of Dedham, then called Contentment.

As the decades and centuries passed, the outermost settlements broke off into their own townships first; they were, after all, far from Dedham center and its Church of Christ, the heart of the colony. By the mid-nineteenth century, only today's Norwood and Westwood remained attached to the mother town. South Dedham, also known as the South Parish or Second Parish, had grown into a village with its own distinct character. What there was of a village square had grown haphazardly with stately homes, retail stores, blacksmiths and stables, a tavern and hall all standing alongside one another. Still, there was a flourishing ink mill and two substantial tanneries that drew new residents, many of them immigrants, and formed the commercial base for independence.

By the time Norwood was incorporated, in 1872, the community was ready to stand on its own. And yet, the town's central business district – known as "the Hook" for the large hitching post where travelers and coach drivers had tied their horses – remained unattractive. For the next half century, bit by bit this area was remade. Wooden buildings and houses, many of which doubled as tin shops and dry goods stores, were razed or moved to make way for brick commercial buildings; the main roadway, known as the Norfolk and Bristol Turnpike, was widened and paved. The railroad arrived and, later, trolley tracks were installed. The old growth trees that shaded the streets were replaced by lampposts and telephone poles. Two large book manufacturing concerns, the Norwood Press and the Plimpton Press, arrived, joining the Winslow Brothers & Smith tannery and the Morrill Ink Company to employ hundreds. Gradually, what once was a village became a cohesive town.

The postcards that follow collectively tell the history of this community from its founding to the end of the twentieth century. The commercial retail district, educational and health care facilities, and recreational activities are all represented as are many of the businesses and industries that were responsible for the town's growth and prosperity. Norwood's public buildings and landmarks also have a place here. Perhaps new to some are the homes – both grand and modest – that were constructed along the streets and avenues of town. The range of domiciles, which include mansions, middle class homes, boardinghouses and apartment buildings, confirm that Norwood was always a community with residents of varied economic circumstances. Similarly, the houses of worship pictured here provide further proof of the ethnic and religious diversity that characterized the town in the early twentieth century and continues to this day.

Postcards themselves have a fascinating history. Production proliferated in the late 1800s and early 1900s, first with cards printed in Germany; later they were produced domestically, and even locally. It was not until 1907 that postcards were allowed to bear messages on the left side of the card's back. Prior to that date, the entire back of the postcard was reserved for the address only. Thus, many early cards have short messages scribbled on the front of the card – the "text message" of the age.

The cards themselves ranged from unique "real photo" postcards, to grainy black and white images, to hand-colored and eventually, by the mid-twentieth century, brilliant-colored views. Although they are still mass-produced today (used primarily as souvenirs rather than communication), the "Golden Age" of postcards is considered between 1900 and 1930. The majority of the images in this book come from that period.

It is a pleasure to share this collection of postcards with a new audience. For many, these views will spark nostalgia for the past; for others, they record totally unfamiliar places and structures. Either way, this was vintage Norwood.

One

FROM VILLAGE TO TOWN

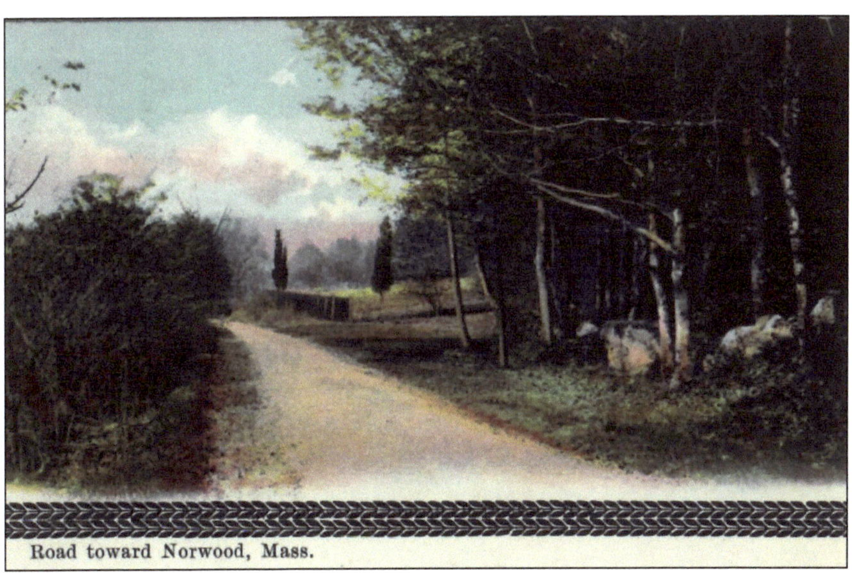

As colonists ventured beyond Dedham, the trails once traversed only by Native peoples became well-worn roadways. South Dedham, known as Tiot, was one of the last districts to break away from its mother town. The road to Norwood remained a rural way for some time.

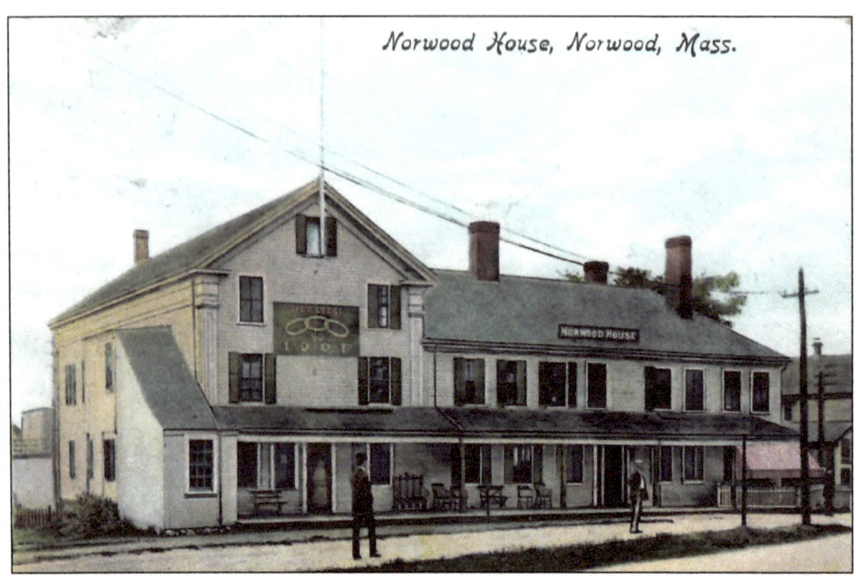

Tiot Tavern, circa 1798, was an important stop on early stagecoach routes. Outside its doors, a tether for horses gave the meagre center its name: "The Hook." Later known as the Norwood Hotel and the Norwood House, it continued to provide food and lodging into the twentieth century.

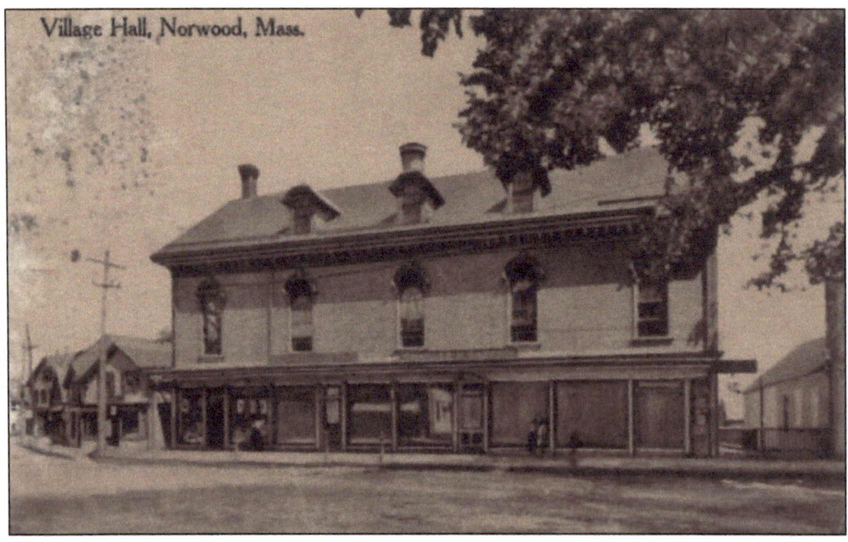

Village Hall, a three-story wooden Italianate-style structure, was erected in the mid-nineteenth century near today's intersection of East Cottage and Washington Streets. It housed retail businesses at street level. The large second floor hall held graduations, fraternal organizational meetings, and community gatherings.

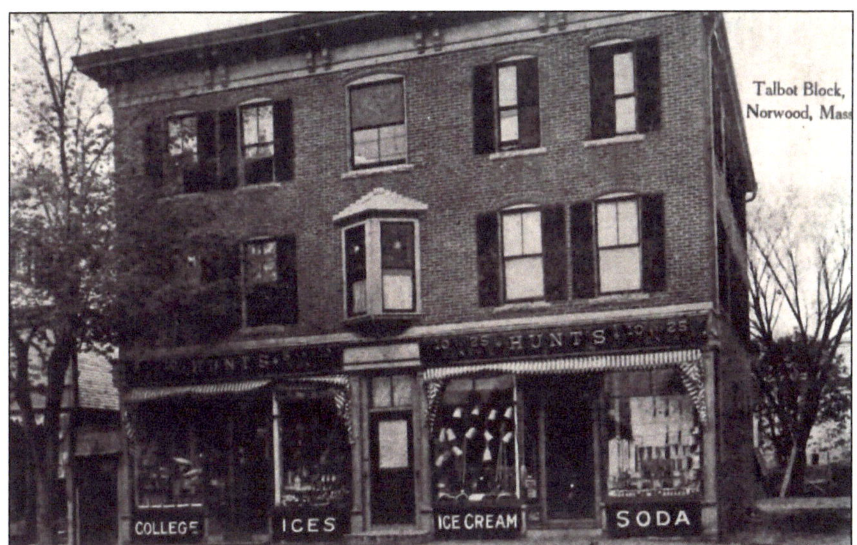

Known locally as "the first Talbot Block," this was one of Norwood's earliest dedicated commercial buildings, going up around 1890. It was situated on the west side of Washington Street between Nahatan and Cottage Streets. For a time, the building was home to the Norwood Clothing Company. Owned and operated by Norwood residents Eugene Sullivan and George Corbett, it was reported to be "the oldest, largest, and most reliable clothing store in town." Eventually outgrowing its quarters at the Talbot Block, the store moved to the Sanborn Block. Later, Hunt's Five and Ten Cent Store opened its doors here. In addition to traditional five and dime store merchandise, Hunt's sold soda and ice cream. By 1918, Hunt's was no longer in Norwood.

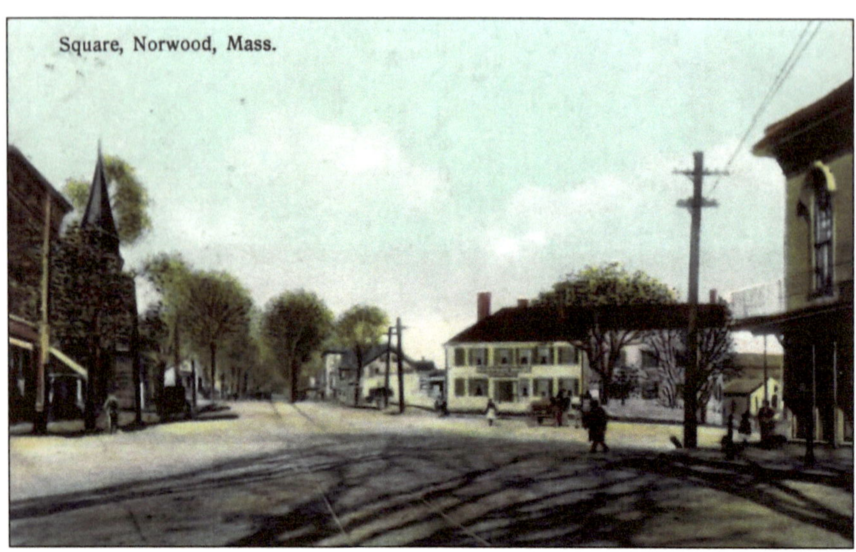

This postcard captures Norwood's square just before large commercial buildings began to dominate the area. To the left, the first Talbot Block and the second Universalist Church can be seen. The Norwood House is at the center, and Village Hall is just visible at the right.

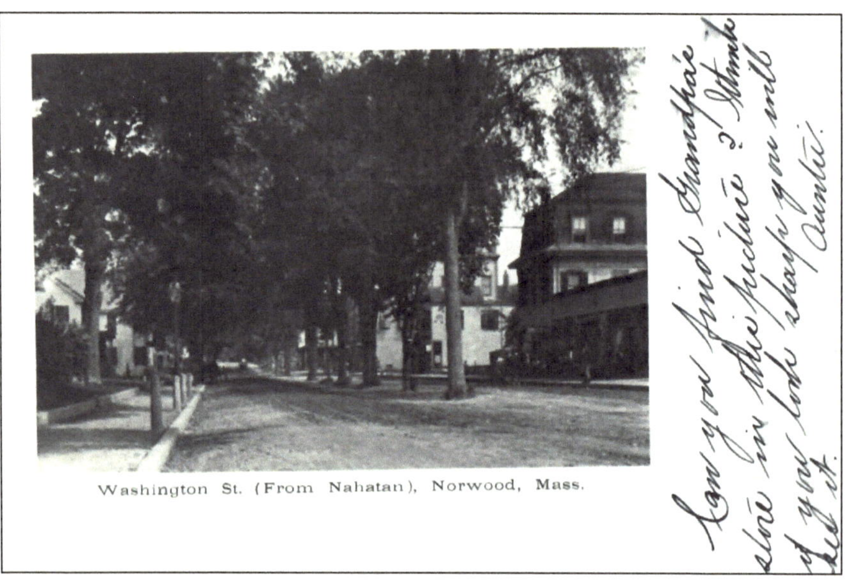

In this view, mailed in 1905, Norwood retains its small-town appearance as mature trees shade the unpaved main street. The sender has written: "Can you find Grandpa's store in the picture? I think if you look sharp you will see it." Whose store she is referring to is unknown.

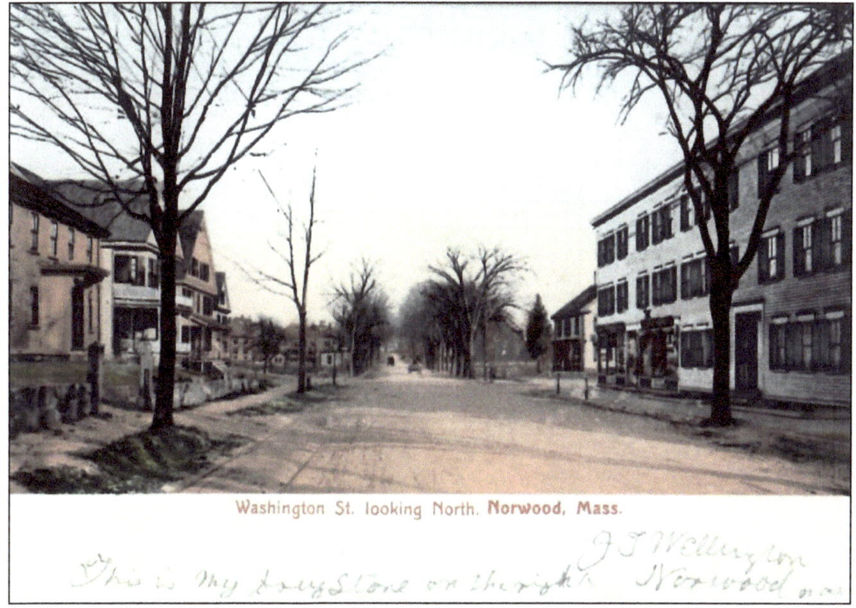

Around 1899, James Hawkins built the commercial block that bore his name at Washington and East Hoyle Streets. It contained retail, office, and living space. Known after 1906 as the Babcock Block and later as the Carberry Block, the building (on right) still stands today.

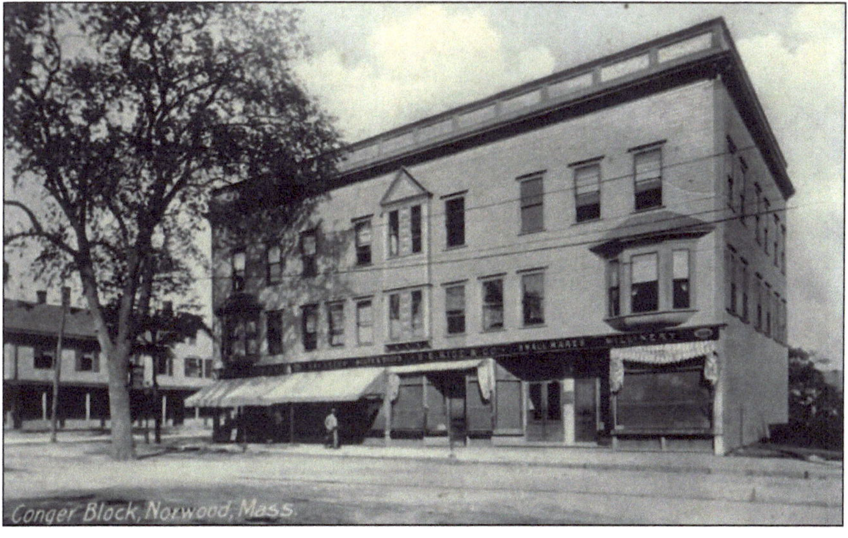

A landmark for decades at the corner of Railroad Avenue and Washington Street, the three-story Conger Block was built in 1895 by James Conger. H. E. Rice operated a successful department store there from 1898 until 1930. Later, it was home to Clark's Pharmacy.

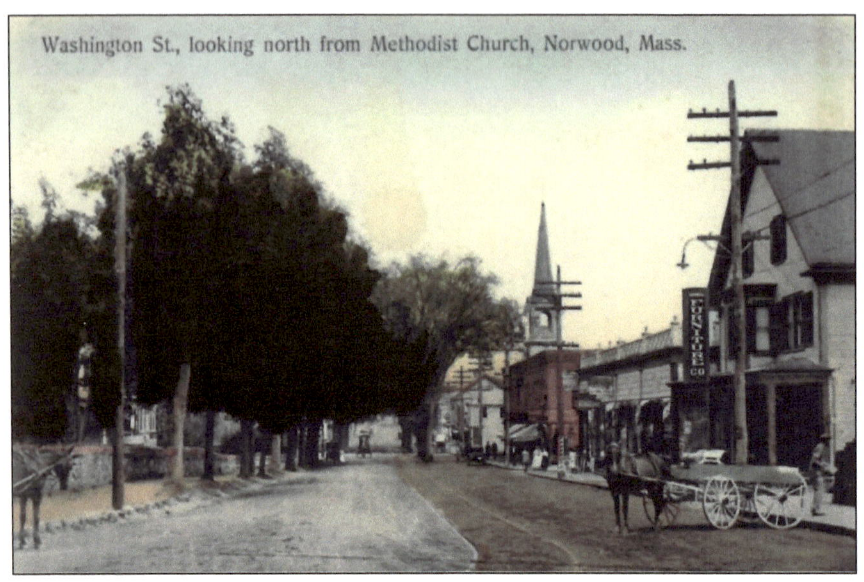

Two images looking north on Washington Street demonstrate the incongruities of the early twentieth century. Above, a horse and wagon stand next to the modern trolley tracks, wooden structures are adjacent to brick commercial buildings. Beside the mature elms, below, stand newly-installed telephone and electric light poles. The First Baptist Church, dedicated in 1859, overlook both scenes.

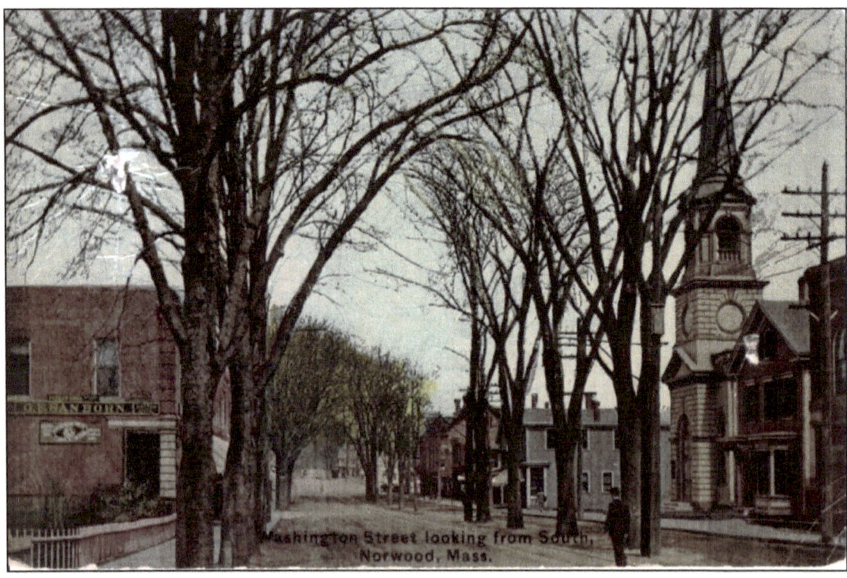

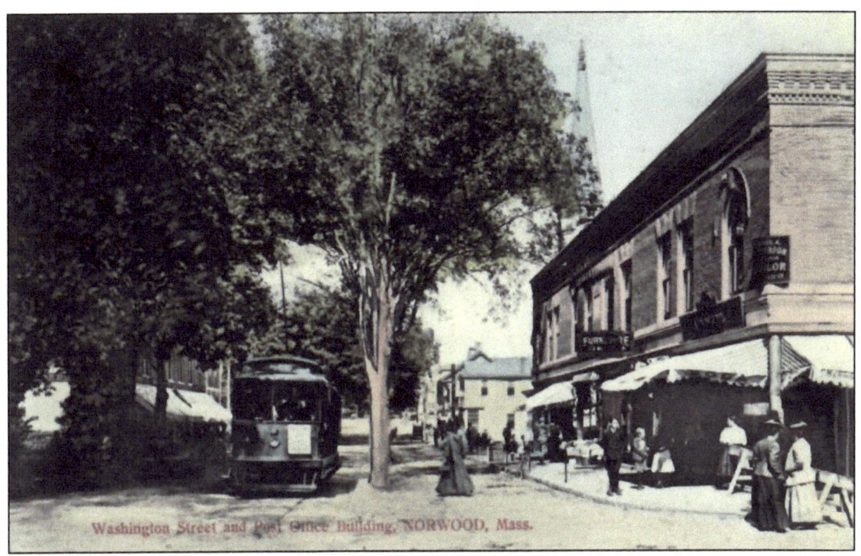

In 1853, Lyman Waldo Bigelow opened a dry goods store in Village Hall. In 1899 it was Bigelow's sons who built the Bigelow Block, seen here. For a number of years, the post office was located in the building. It still stands today at Day and Washington Streets.

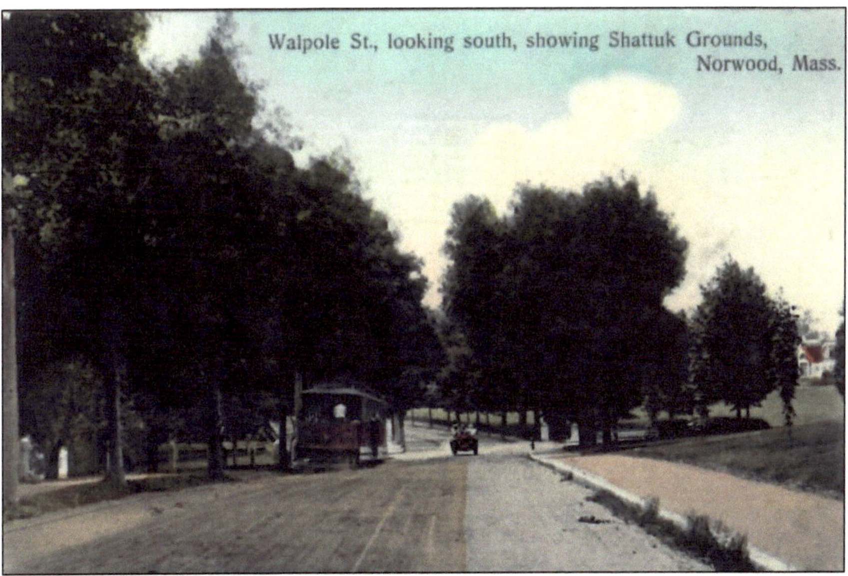

Although it seems a bucolic setting, the modern age is depicted in this image of Walpole Street near the intersection of Winter Street. On the left, a trolley car makes its way along the old Wrentham Road from Walpole Center into Norwood. On the right, an automobile is traveling.

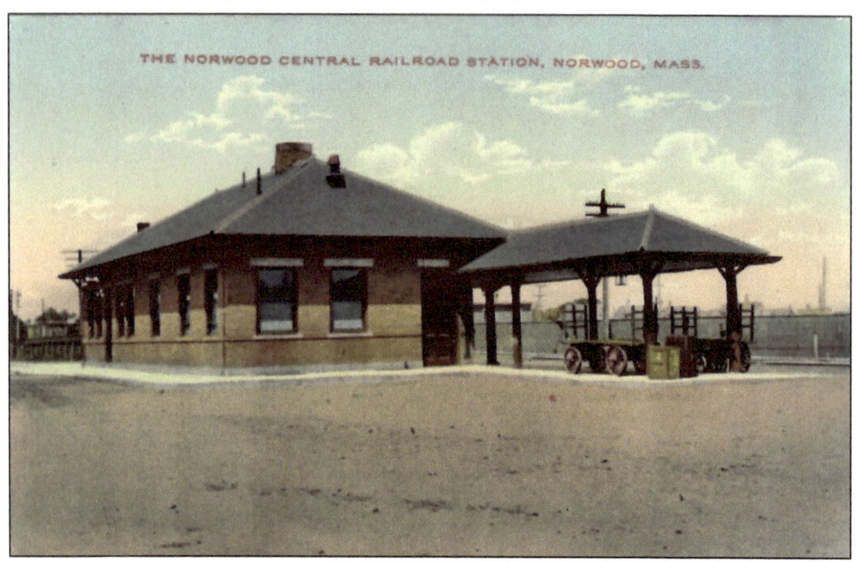

In 1849, the Norfolk County Railroad constructed a line through South Dedham, a sure sign of "progress" for Tiot village, some two decades before its incorporation as Norwood. In the 1890s, Norwood had five stations: Ellis, Norwood Station, Norwood Central, Winslow's, and Morrill's. This is Norwood Central.

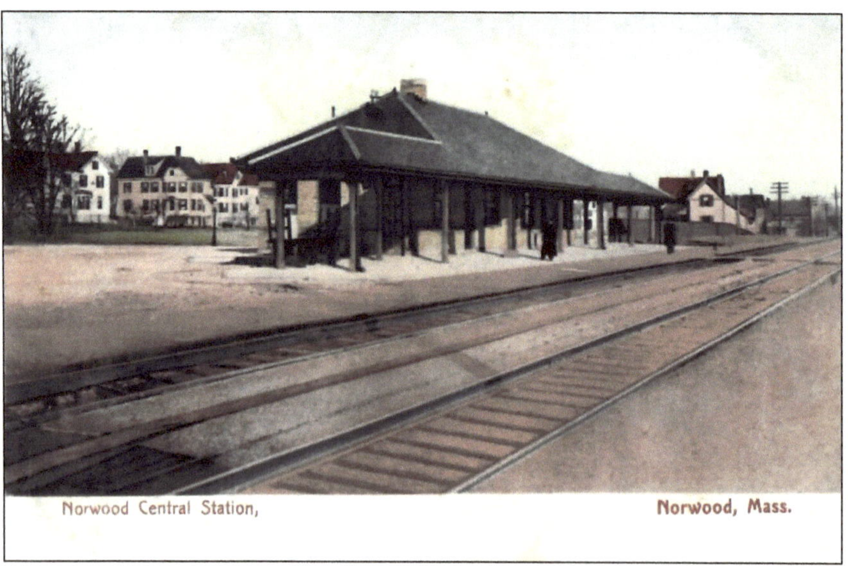

In 1899, this brick train depot building replaced the original wooden Norwood Central station which had been erected in 1865 to serve the New York and New England Railroad line. It served the community for nearly a century before it was taken out of service. The structure still stands.

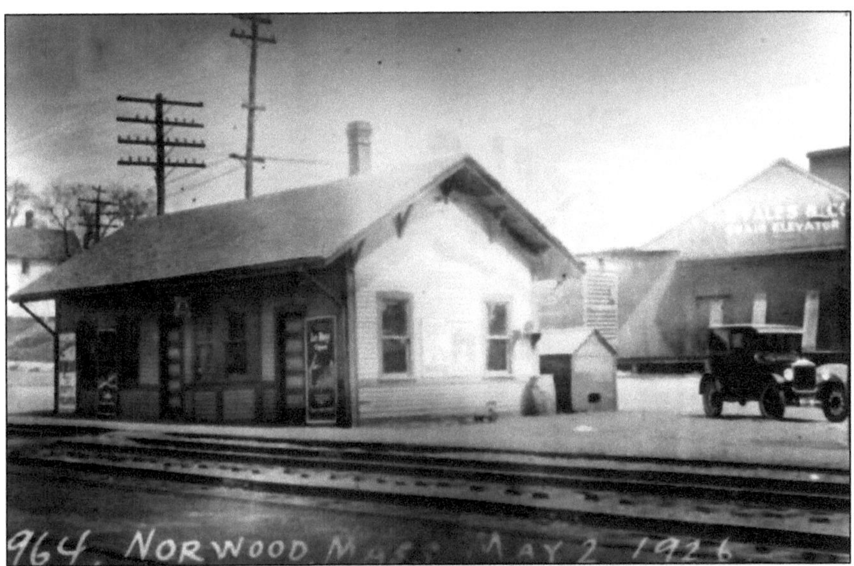

The Norfolk County Railroad line was operated by the New York and New England Railway; the New England Railway; and the New York, New Haven and Hartford Company in succession. The Norwood Station, today's Norwood Depot, stood at Railroad Avenue. The Frank A. Fales & Company, a flour, grain, hay, and feed business seen here, was situated close by the station on Hill Street. In 1908, Fales added lime and cement to its stock. Highly successful, Fales' mill was destroyed by a devastating fire in April of 1931.

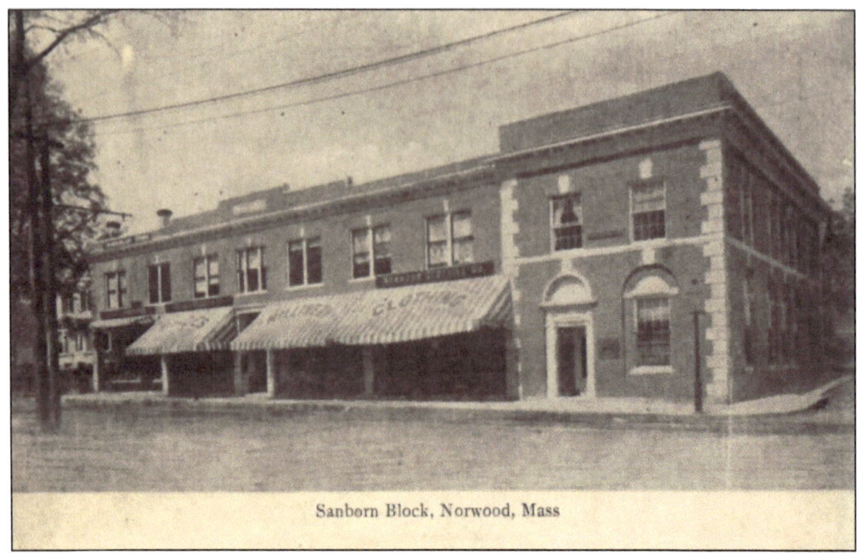

Sanborn Block, Norwood, Mass

Named for George Sanborn, the Sanborn Building was erected in 1907 on the west side of Washington Street between Day and Vernon Streets. Born in South Dedham, Sanborn was a clerk, then owner of a hardware store. After this handsome block was built, he moved his retail business here.

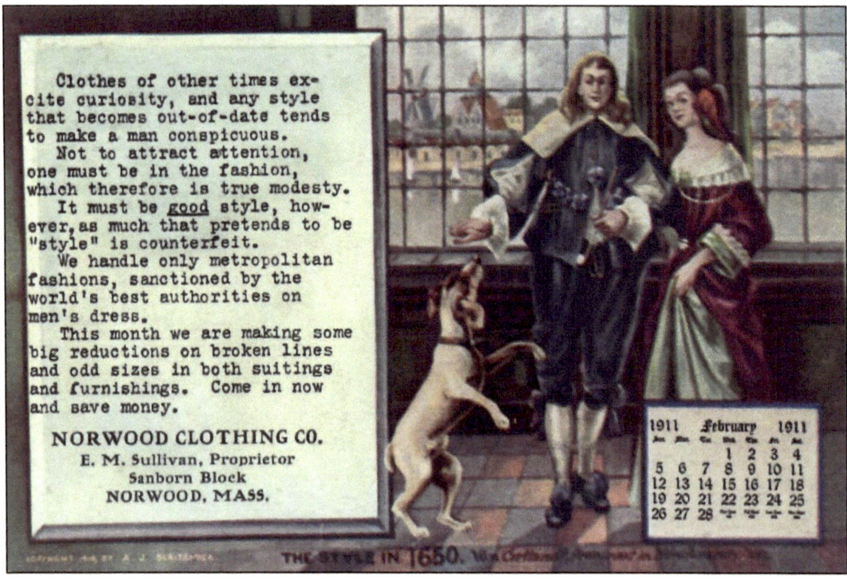

The Norwood Clothing Company, founded by Norwood residents George Corbett and Eugene Sullivan, was originally located in the first Talbot Block. It was later relocated into the more spacious Sanborn Block. In 1911, when this postcard was distributed, Sullivan was the store's sole proprietor.

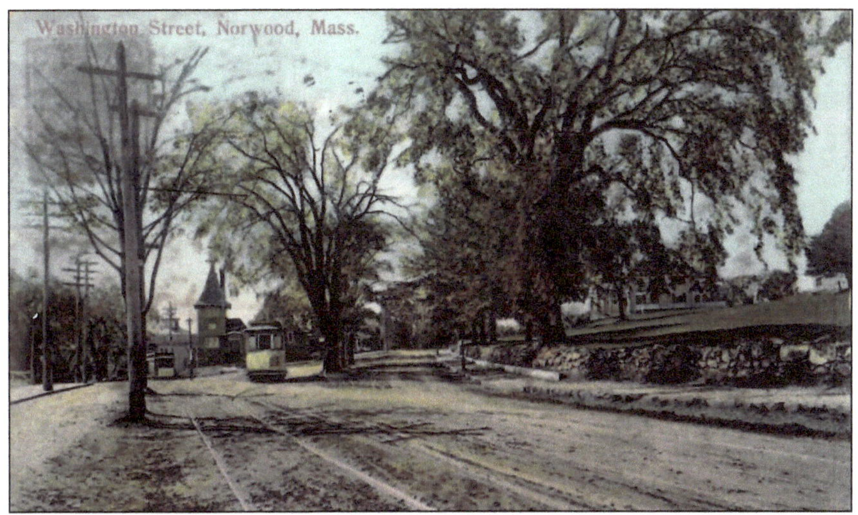

Originally called the Wrentham Road, the roadway that follows today's Walpole Street (Route 1A) opened in 1751. Seen here is the junction of Walpole and Washington Streets where the Wrentham Road bears to the right and continues to Walpole, Wrentham, and beyond.

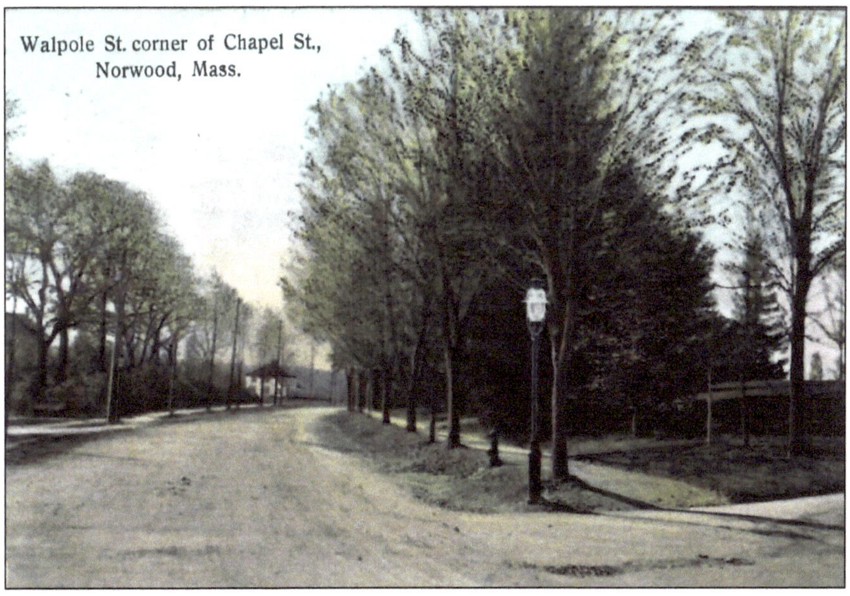

Farther south on the Wrentham Road is the park at Walpole and Chapel Streets. Initially a few acres of woodland, it was donated to the town by the Winslow family and was known as Winslow Park until rededicated as the Disabled American Veterans Memorial Park.

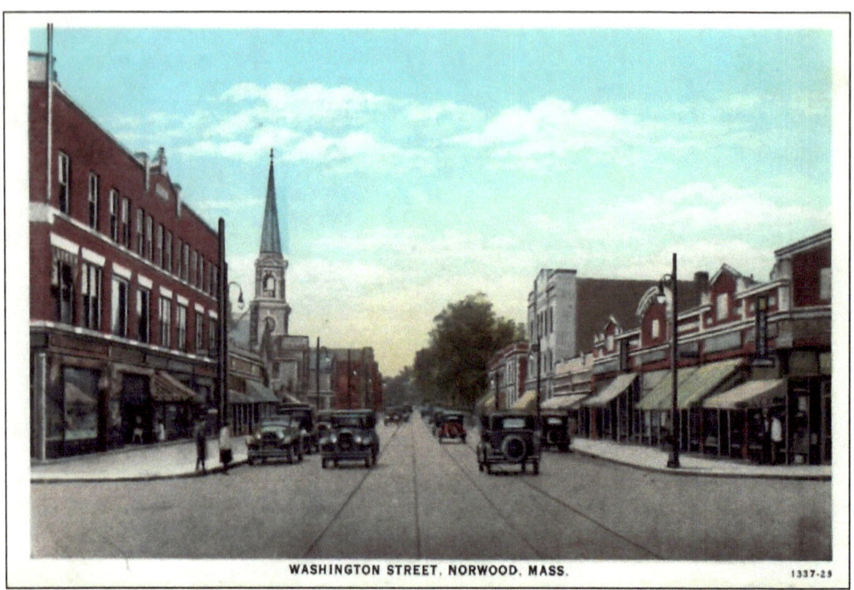

Born in South Dedham in 1865, James Folan worked at various occupations before opening a successful shoe store. He was responsible for the red brick Folan Block erected at East Cottage and Washington Streets in 1916. The venerable Village Hall was moved to allow for its construction.

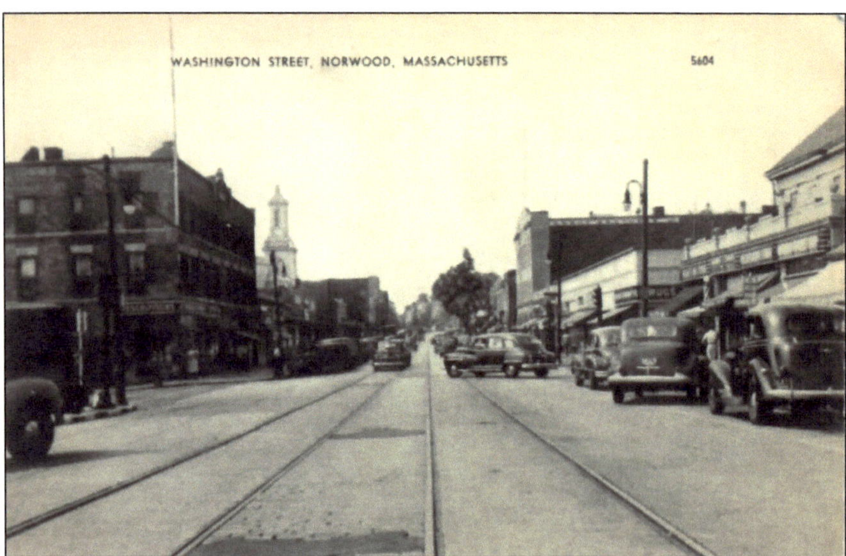

This image, taken years later from virtually the same location as above, shows an unchanged Folan building. But the First Baptist Church, visible farther south, has been altered. The original steeple, severely damaged during the hurricane of 1938, was replaced.

18

Two

EDUCATION

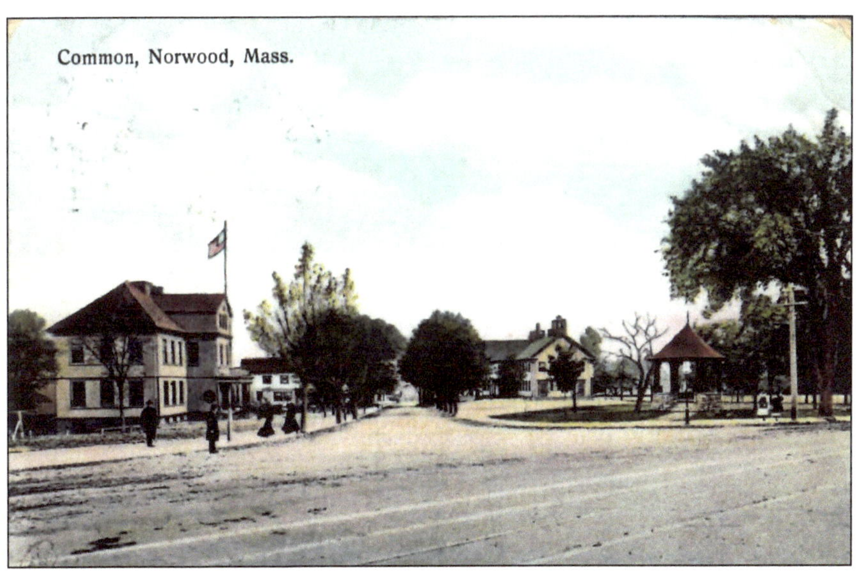

This view from the top of Guild Street, captures Guild Square including the Guild School (left), built in 1894; the Everett School (back center), built in 1851 when the village was still part of Dedham; and the Bandstand (right), erected c.1903 for community entertainments.

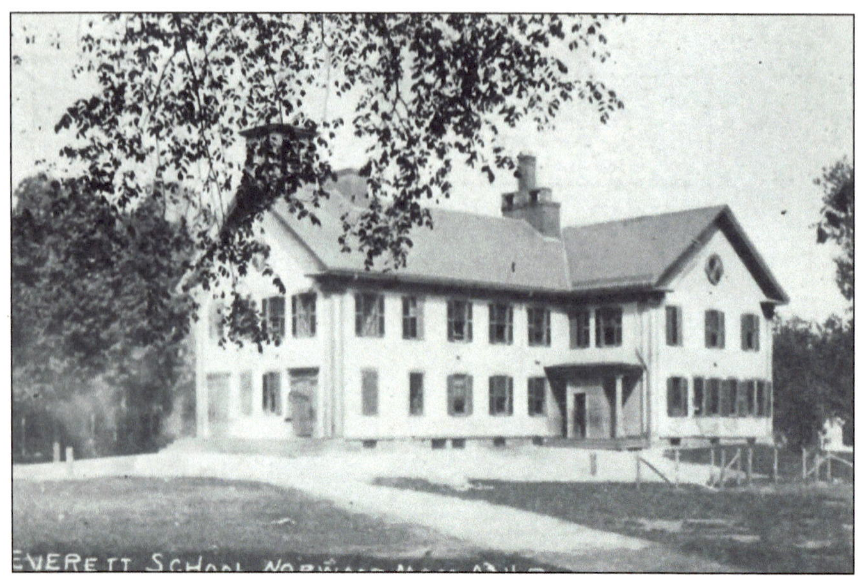

The Everett School was dedicated in December 1851 when Norwood was still part of Dedham. Named after Israel Everett, a Dedham native and veteran of the Battle of Bunker Hill, it was originally a two-room schoolhouse. North and south wings were added during the 1860s.

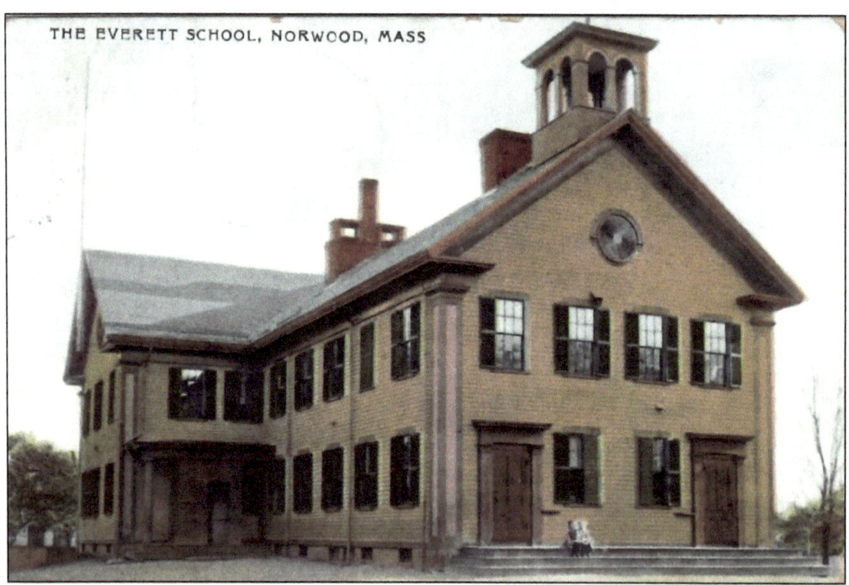

Regarded as the best of Dedham's schools when it opened, the Everett School bordered the Guild Park on today's Central Street. The school was taken out of service and razed in 1930 to be replaced by the U.S. Post Office, built in 1933.

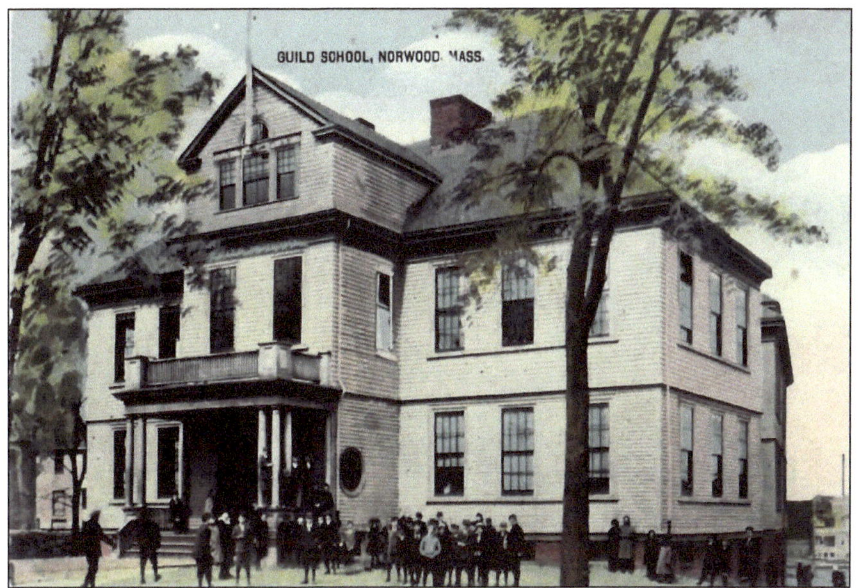

The Guild School, built in 1894, stood near the corner of Guild and Central Streets, on land that had once belonged to the Moses Guild family. Five years later, an addition was needed; the building held grades one through six in twelve classrooms.

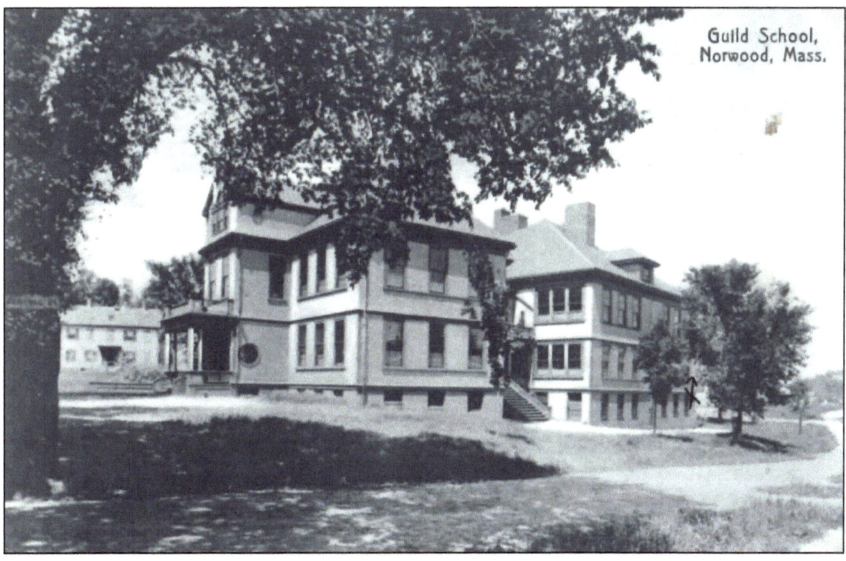

This view of the Guild School captures the addition which doubled the school's size. It was constructed in 1899, by Norwood resident Forrest Douglass at a cost of $8,000. The Guild School was destroyed by fire in 1929.

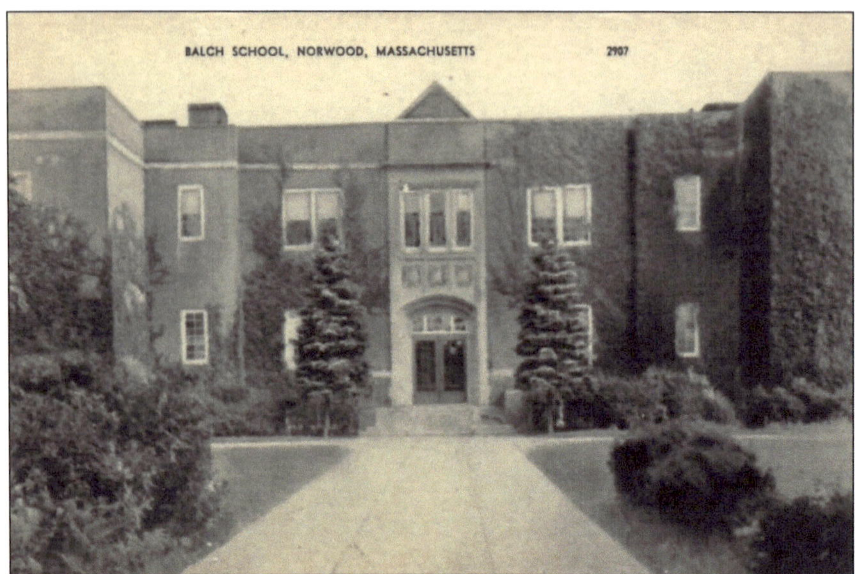

Named in memory of South Dedham's first pastor, Rev. Thomas Balch, the first Balch School was built in 1867 to replace the aging "Old Brick" School that stood farther south at Pleasant and Sumner Streets. This brick structure replaced the original Balch in 1913.

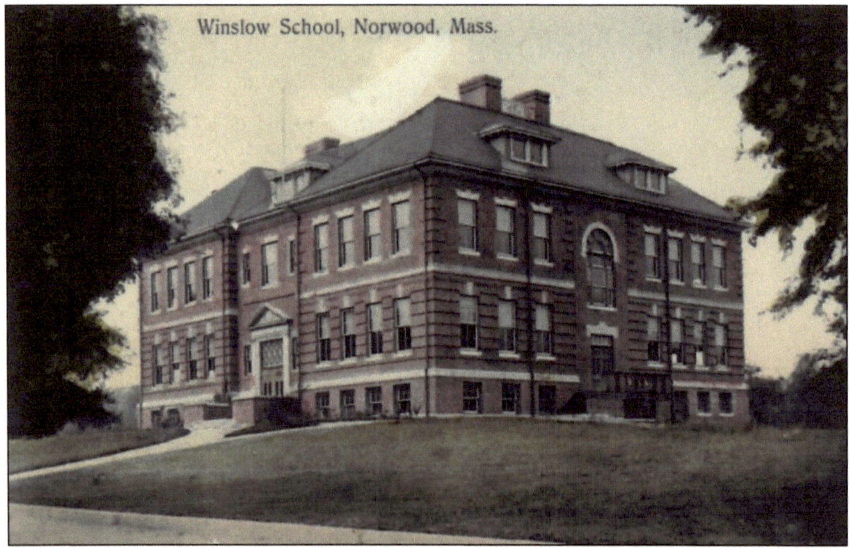

In 1907, the Winslow School, dedicated to the Winslow family, owners of the largest tannery in town, was built at Chapel Street and Winslow Avenue. Its proximity to the Balch, although on opposite sides of the railroad tracks, alleviated some of the overcrowding in that neighborhood school.

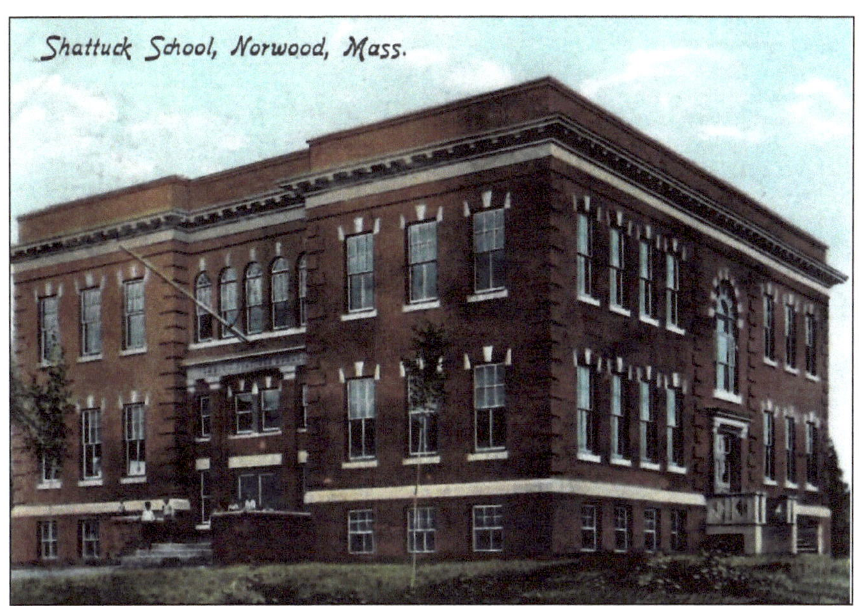

On the northern side of Norwood, the Edmund J. Shattuck Elementary School opened its doors on Fulton Street in 1903. It replaced the North School, which had been hastily erected in 1878 to serve the growing population in that part of town.

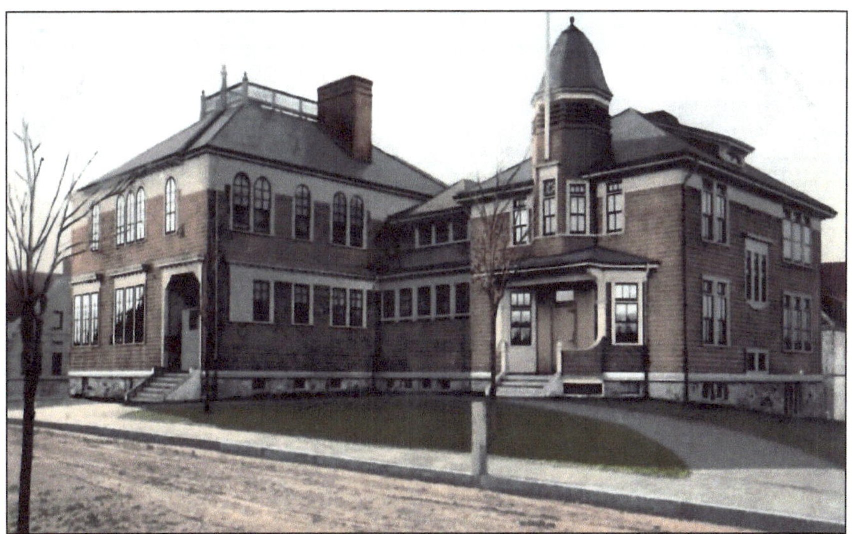

Norwood's first dedicated high school, located on Beacon Hill, opened in 1890. In 1897, the schoolhouse was doubled in size. In 1919, when a new high school was built, it became a grade school, renamed the Beacon School. The building was demolished in 1942.

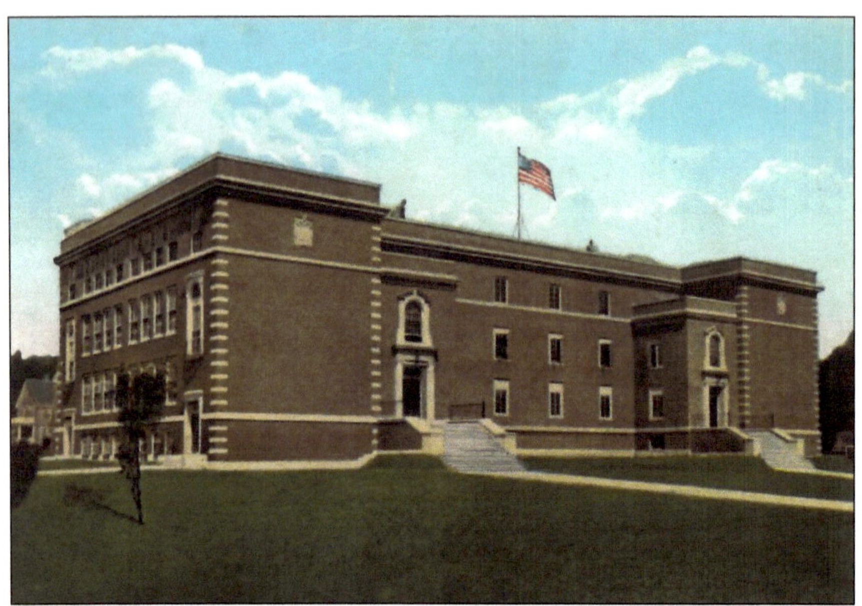

At a cost of more than $300,000, a new combination junior and senior high school was opened in 1919 on Washington Street, across from the Norwood Civic Association. Its completion enabled the school department to offer both college preparation and vocational classes.

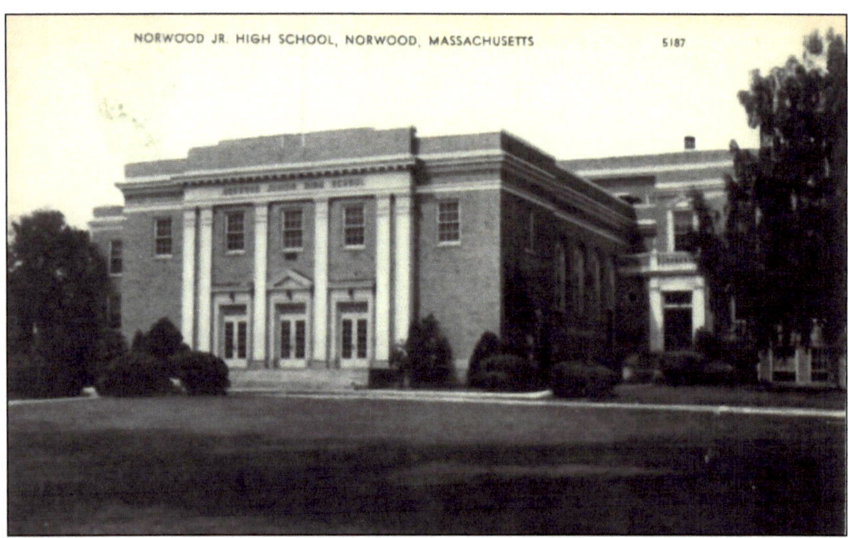

Shortly after a 1921 addition, the junior/senior high school was once again overcrowded. A new senior high was built, making this facility a junior high. Following a fire in 1971, the building was converted into an elementary school. It is now the Guild Medical Building.

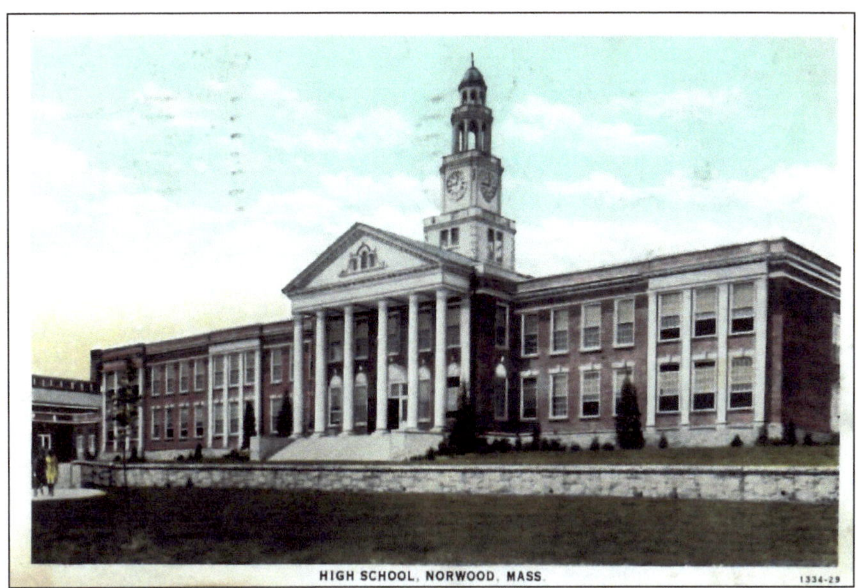

Built on a 15-acre plot of land donated by local philanthropists George F. Willett and Frank Allen, the third Norwood Senior High stood on Nichols Street. The architect was Norwood native William G. Upham. The red brick Neo-Federal building with a central columned portico and clock tower opened in 1926.

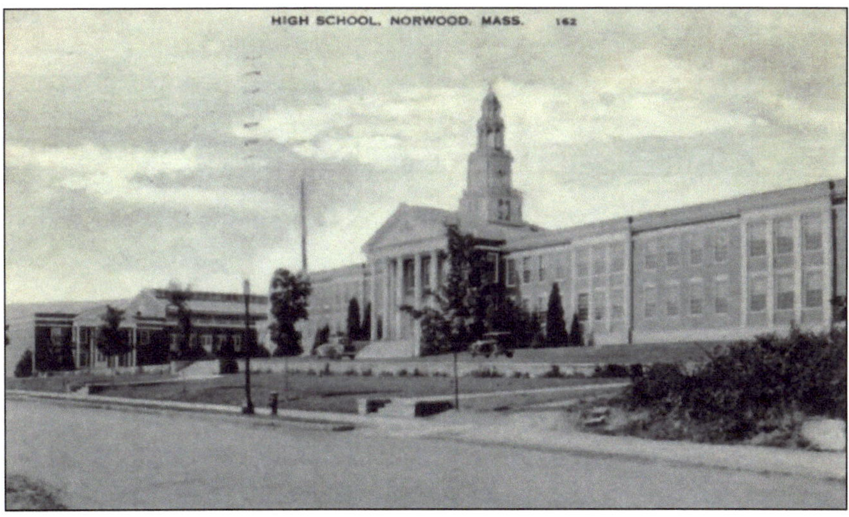

Norwood's Senior High School drew immediate praise for its aesthetic appeal as well as its modern educational features. Only five years later, it was enlarged with a complementary wing, seen in this postcard, to the left of the main structure.

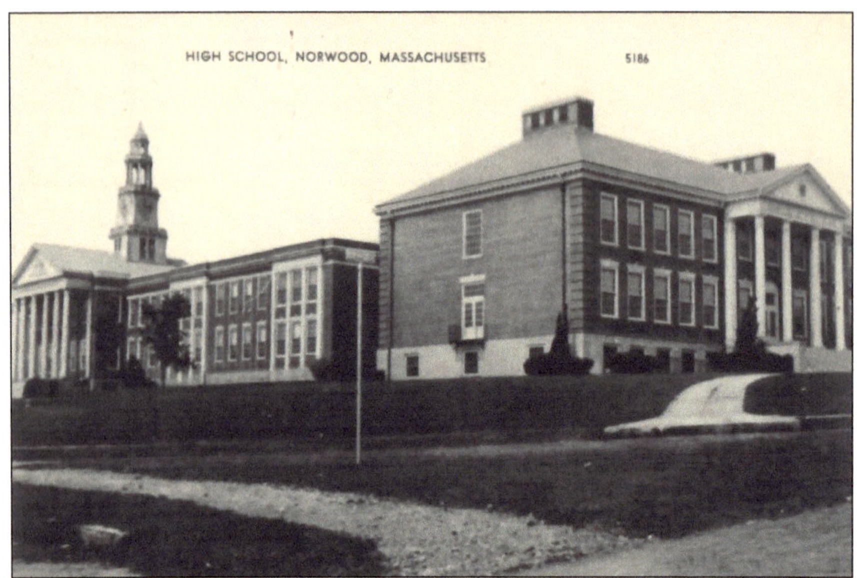

Monies left by Henry O. Peabody to construct a vocational school were utilized to erect the Henry O. Peabody School for Girls. Housed on the Norwood Senior High School campus in a building which complemented the existing structure, the school, visible on the right, opened in September 1942.

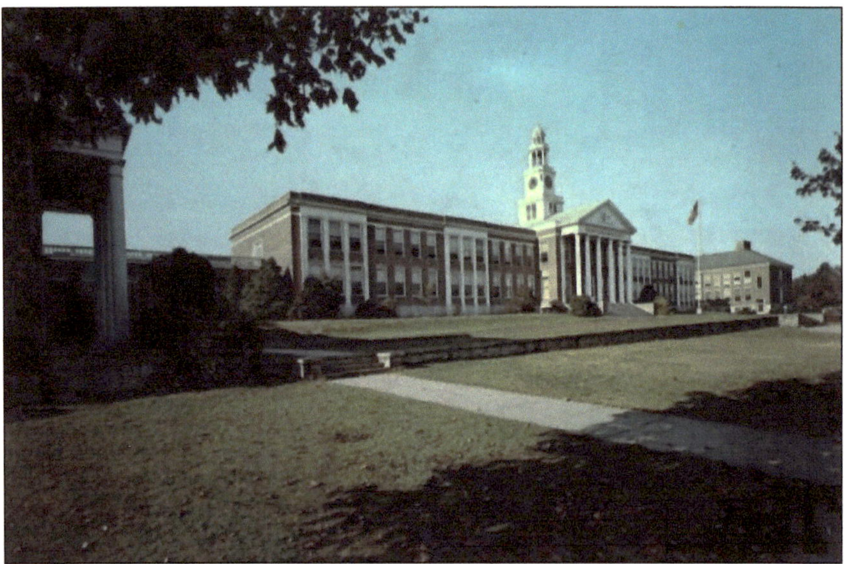

One of Norwood's most beloved structures, the Norwood Senior High School, after a number of additions and upgrades, was ultimately replaced by a new high school building in 2011. Hundreds of graduates returned for a "Last Hurrah" celebration to bid farewell to this iconic "School on the Hill."

Three

HEALTH

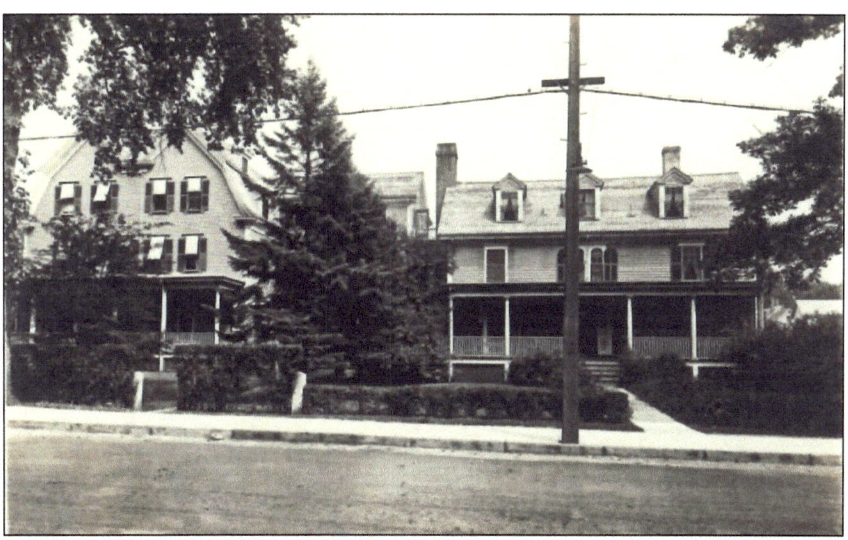

In 1902, Dr. Eben Norton opened a private hospital in his home on Washington Street. In 1913, George F. Willett purchased the property and attached a larger house to the existing "hospital." Willett's plan was to have a public health care facility open to all.

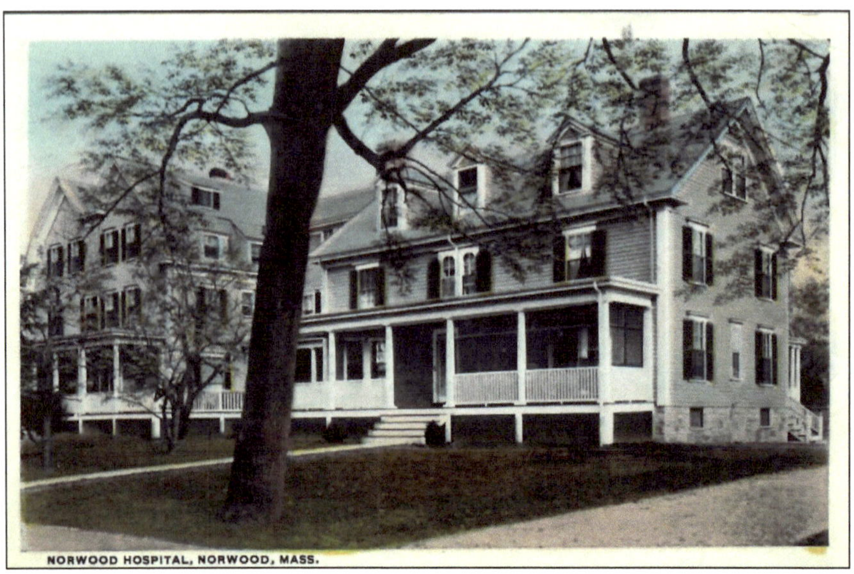

Norwood's first health center contained men's and women's wards, an operating room, maternity ward, and nursery. By 1918, the facility had two dozen beds and a nursery for eight infants. In addition, the Center coordinated dental, eye, and tuberculosis clinics, and provided visiting nurses to treat patients at home.

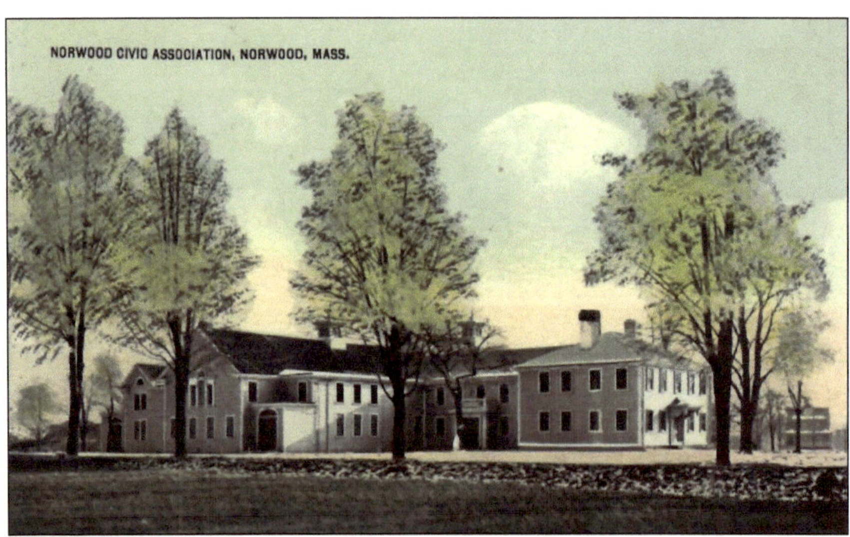

George F. Willett's Norwood Civic Association offered a host of recreational activities to townspeople. When the influenza epidemic of 1918 arrived in Norwood in mid-September, the Civic building was pressed into service as an Emergency Hospital.

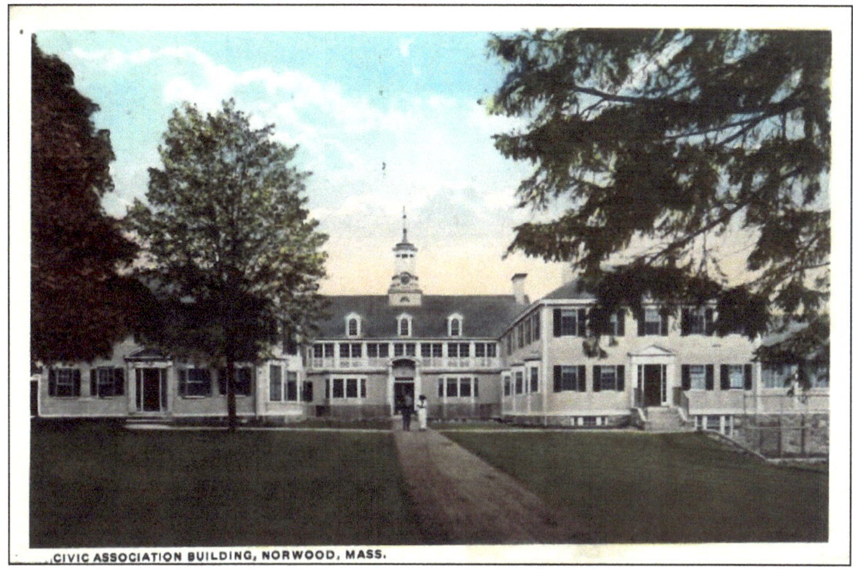

During the 1918 health crisis, the Civic's large second-floor room was made into the women's ward; the first-floor Everett Hall was designated for men. The gymnasium became a morgue. Other rooms were left for supplies, rest areas for volunteers, and housing for medical personnel.

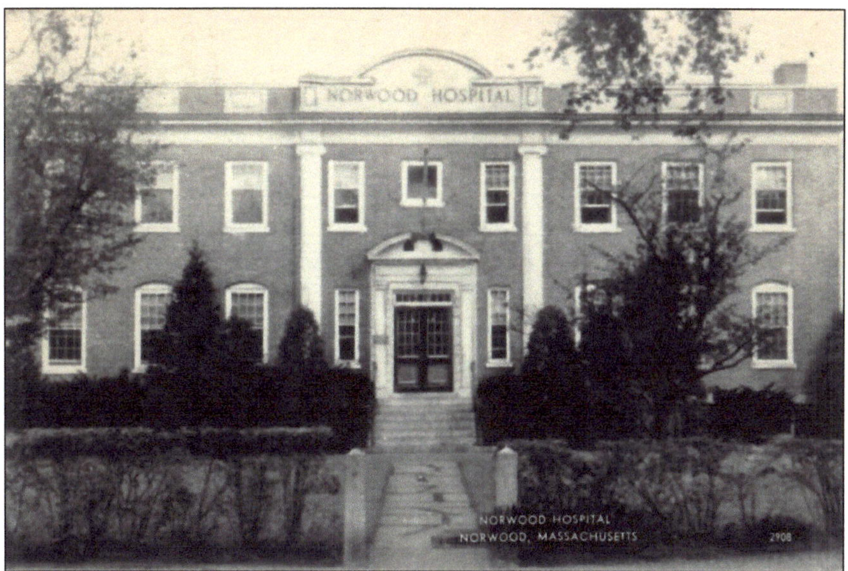

On January 17, 1919, a charter in the name of Norwood Hospital was granted by the Commonwealth of Massachusetts and the corporation took over Willett's cottage hospital. A new brick building was added to the complex in 1928. This building contained offices, a lecture room, and pharmacy.

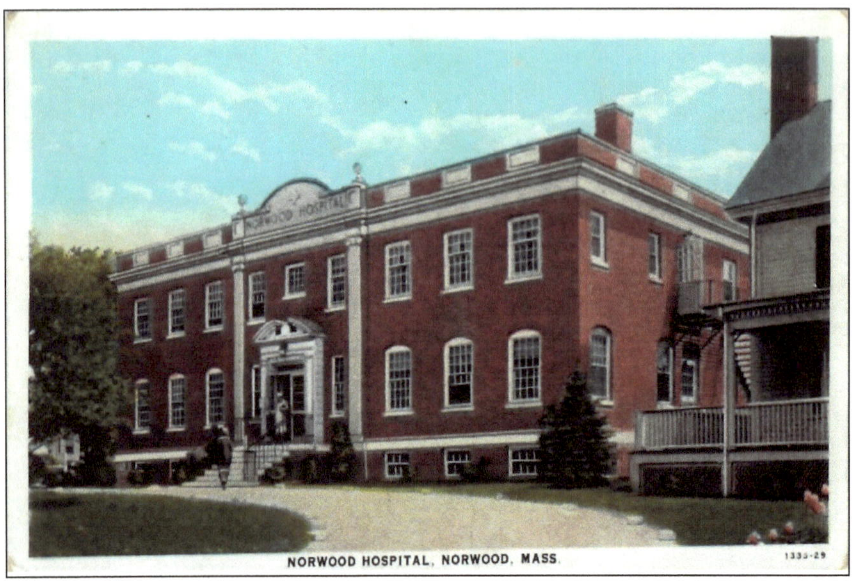

NORWOOD HOSPITAL, NORWOOD, MASS.

The Norwood Hospital quickly elected a Board of Trustees, and a hospital superintendent was appointed. In February of 1928, the public was invited to tour the new hospital building. A portion of the original hospital can be seen to the right in this view.

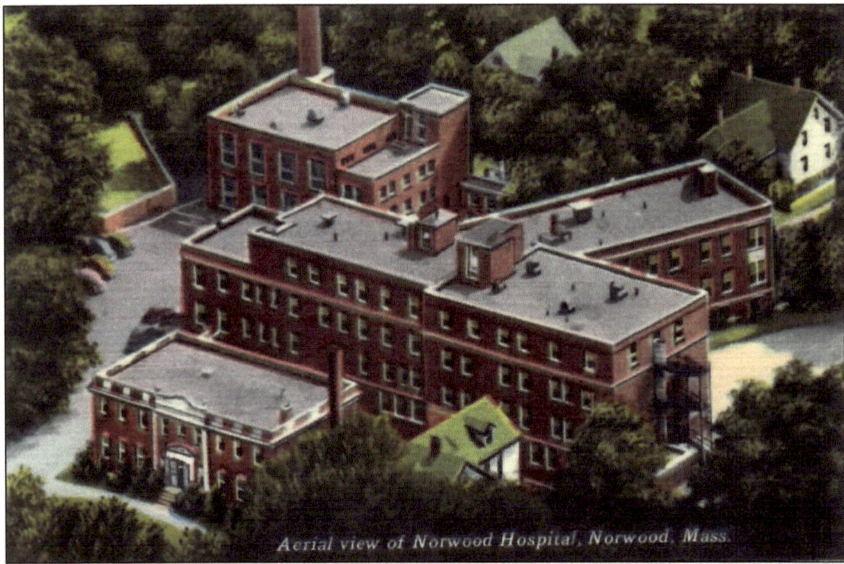

Aerial view of Norwood Hospital, Norwood, Mass.

The Norwood Hospital expanded rapidly: the south wing opened in 1942, a power plant was added in 1949. The east wing opened in 1952, adding 160 beds, enlarged laboratory facilities, operating rooms, the latest in x-ray technology, and an enhanced maternity ward.

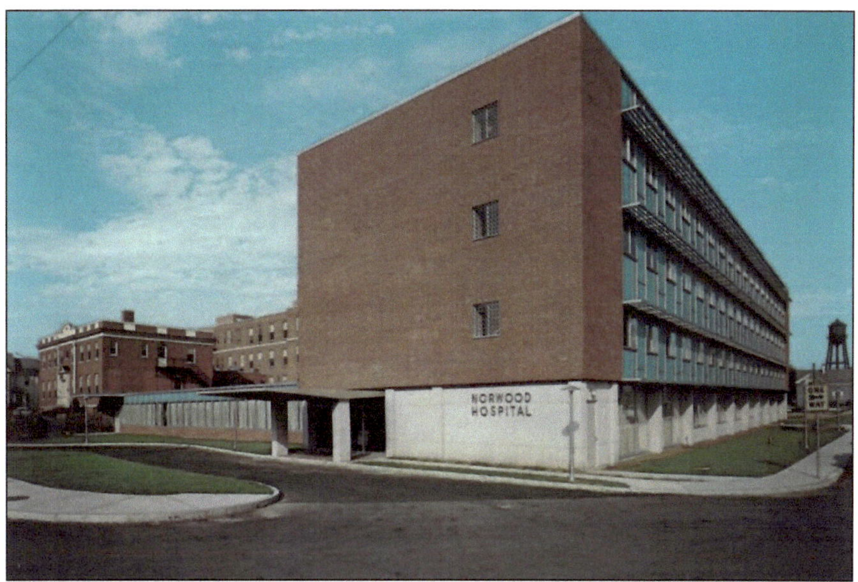

The west wing, a three-story modern structure, was added to the Norwood Hospital complex in 1962. There were now 257 in-patient beds, plus 44 in the maternity ward, a nursery for premature infants, an enlarged x-ray department, and updated operating and recovery rooms.

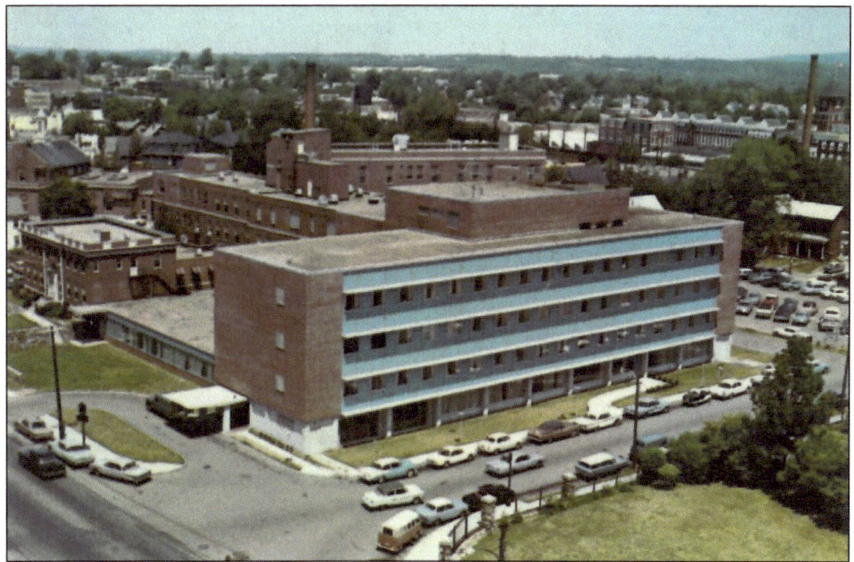

During the 1960s, Norwood Hospital added a ten-bed intensive care and coronary care unit, a bacteriology service, and blood bank office. The hospital's emergency room featured a four-bay, covered ambulance entrance and multiple treatment beds.

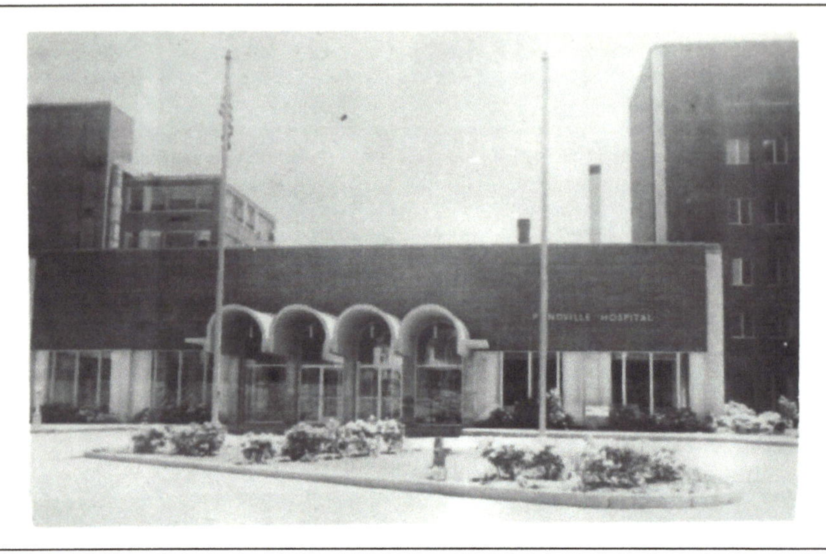

In 1981, the newly-named Neponset Valley Health System acquired the Pondville Hospital. Situated on eighty acres of wooded land in nearby Norfolk, Pondville was founded in 1927 as a cancer care facility. Renamed Southwood Community Hospital in 1982, it remained part of the hospital system until its closure.

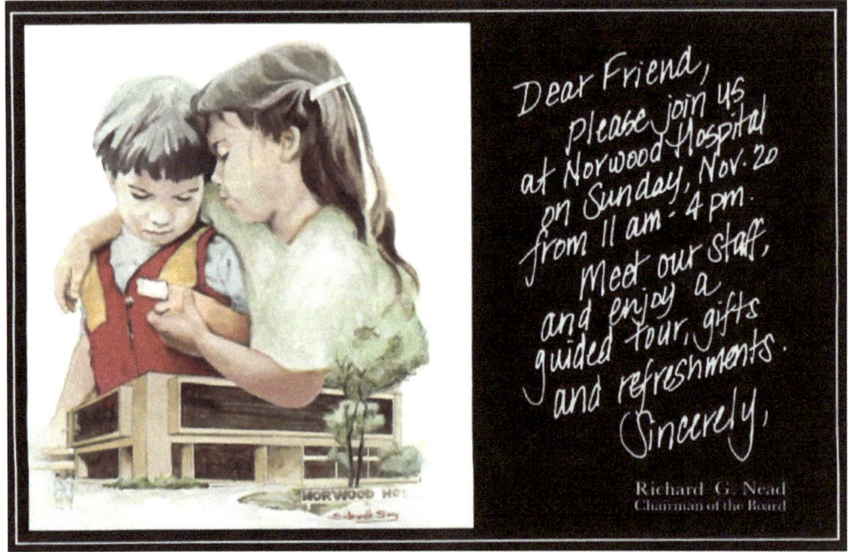

Dedicated in 1983, the Joseph J. Lorusso Building was constructed on the former site of the Norwood Civic Association. Distributed as an invitation to the public, this postcard features a depiction of an original painting created by Boston's famous Sidewalk Sam to commemorate the facility.

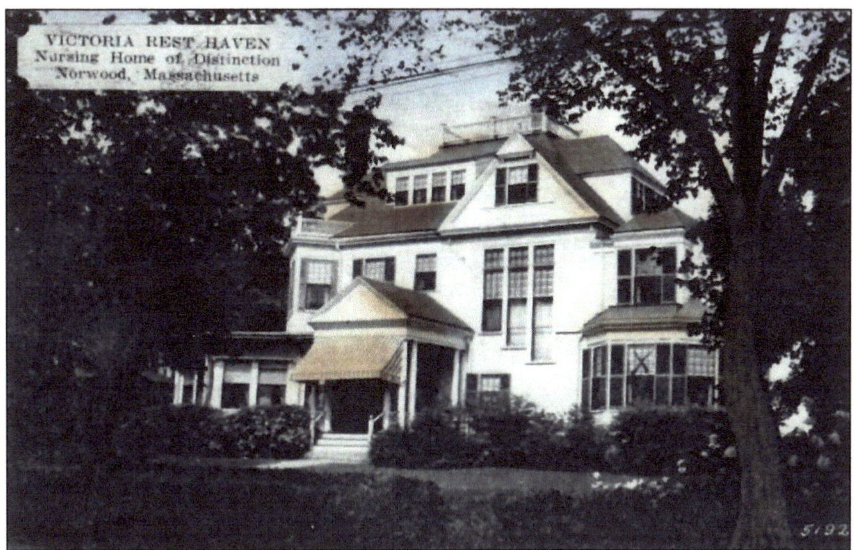

In 1935, the mansion which was once the home of George H. Morrill was converted into a home for the elderly. Still standing on Nichols Street today, the expanded Victoria Haven is a post-surgery rehabilitation and skilled nursing center offering both short- and long-term care.

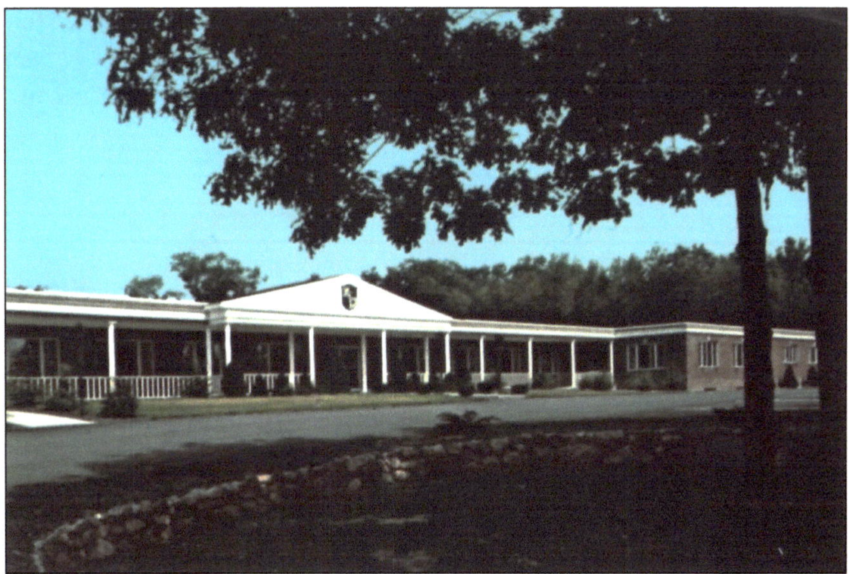

The former Walpole Street home of George F. Willett was converted into a nursing home in 1953. Initially, residents were housed in Willett's former home but, by the late 1960s, the mansion was replaced with a modern, single-story brick structure called "Charlwell House."

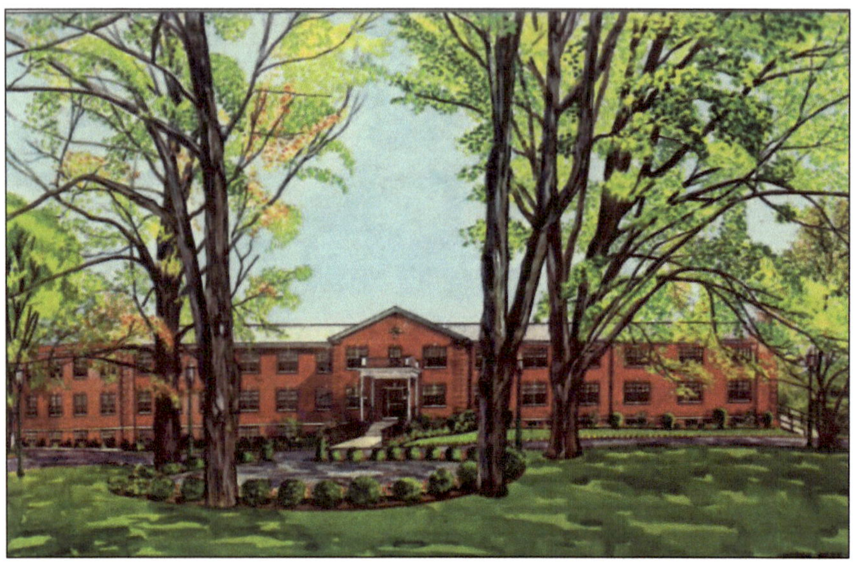

This postcard rendition of the Maple Grove Manor was printed shortly after the facility opened in 1965. Some fifty years later, known as Norwood HealthCare, it offers skilled rehabilitation and long-term care.

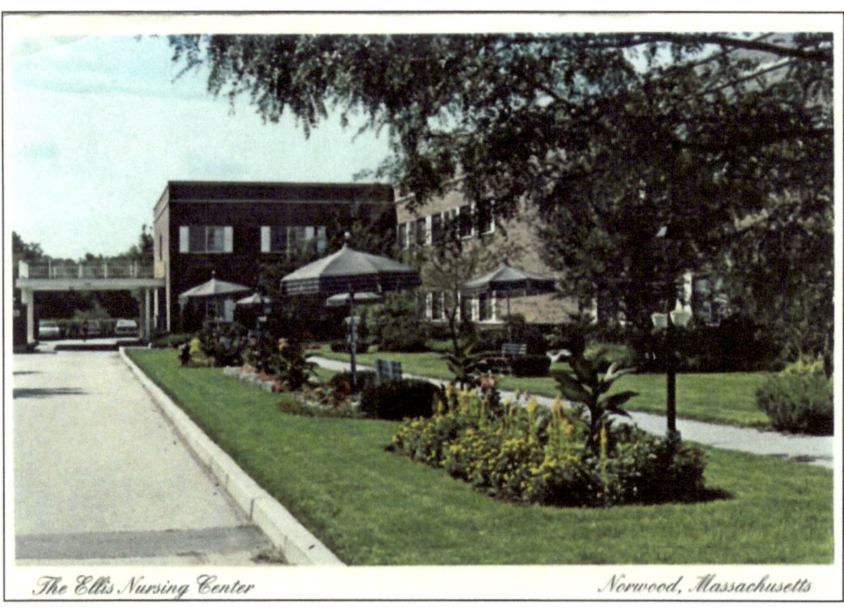

The Ellis Nursing Center has offered short- and long-term orthopedic, cardiac, and pulmonary physical and occupational therapy since 1974. Situated on Ellis Avenue, the building features a rehab gymnasium, chapel, pub and café, and outdoor patio space for its clients.

Four

HOME SWEET HOME

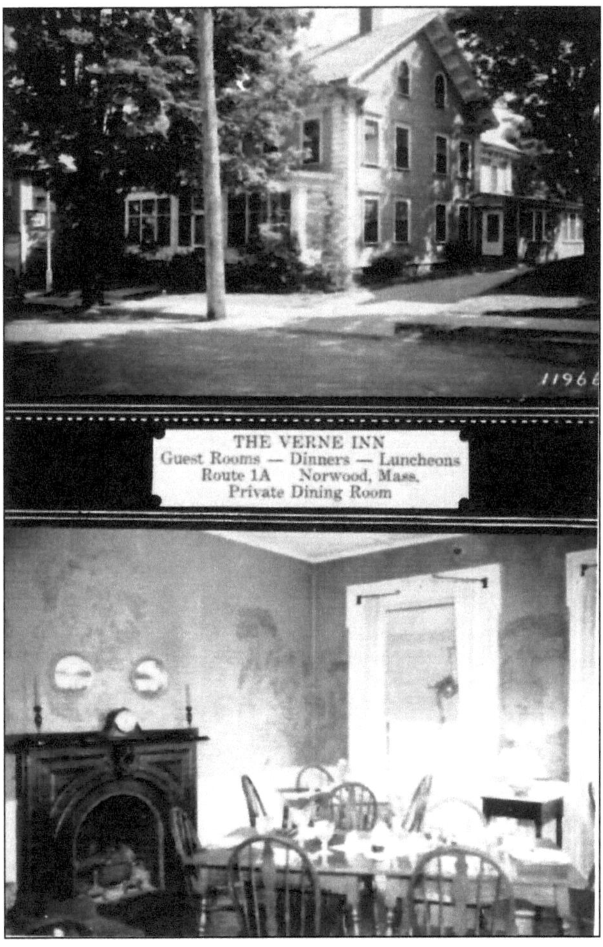

In the early twentieth century, the former home of Joel Baker was moved to Vernon Street where it became The Verne Inn. As this card demonstrates, they served lunch and dinner as well as renting rooms. The building remains a boarding house today.

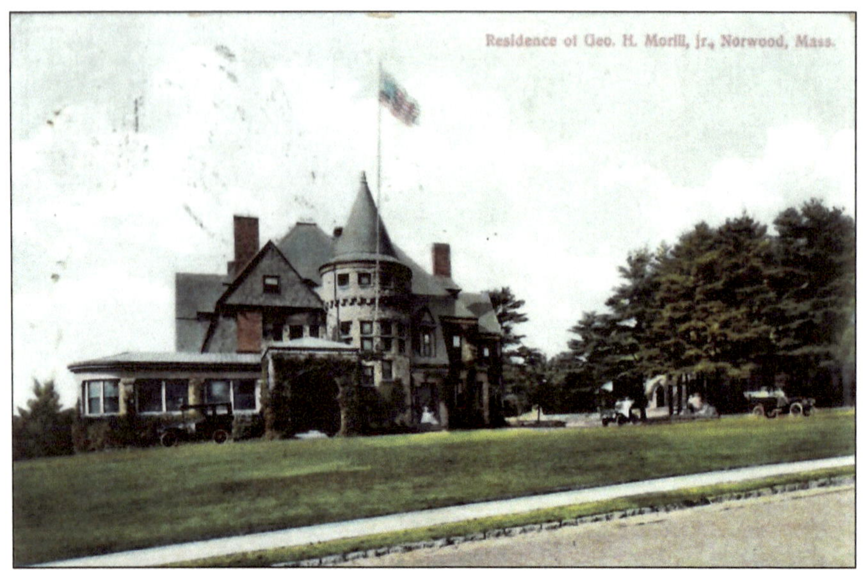

Built in 1890, the magnificent home of George H. Morrill, Jr., called The Pines, stood at the intersection of Bond and Nichols Streets. The castle-like structure eventually fell into disrepair and was demolished in the mid-twentieth century; it was replaced with a development of smaller homes.

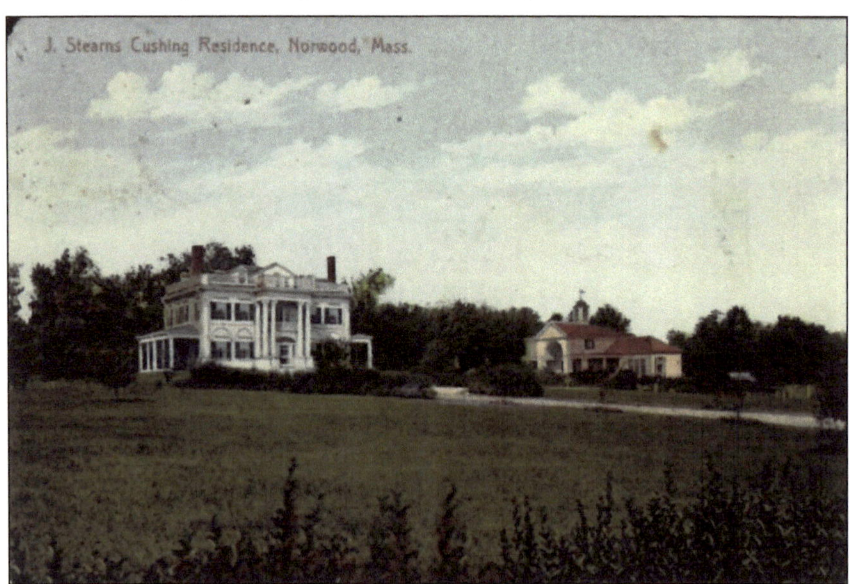

J. Stearns Cushing brought his composition room and electrotype foundry to Norwood in 1894 as part of the Norwood Press. His remarkable Colonial Revival mansion and carriage house stood at the head of Saunders Road. It was demolished in 1996 to make way for a subdivision of homes.

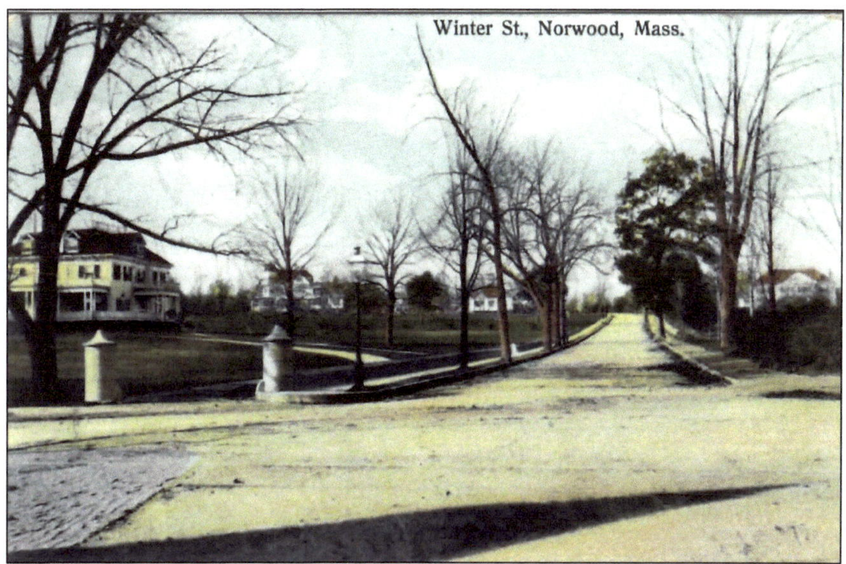

Edmund Shattuck and his wife, Emma Morrill, built this estate at the corner of Winter and Walpole Streets. Their daughter, Maude Shattuck, a long-time library trustee, lived there until her death. It was torn down when the current First Congregational Church was built.

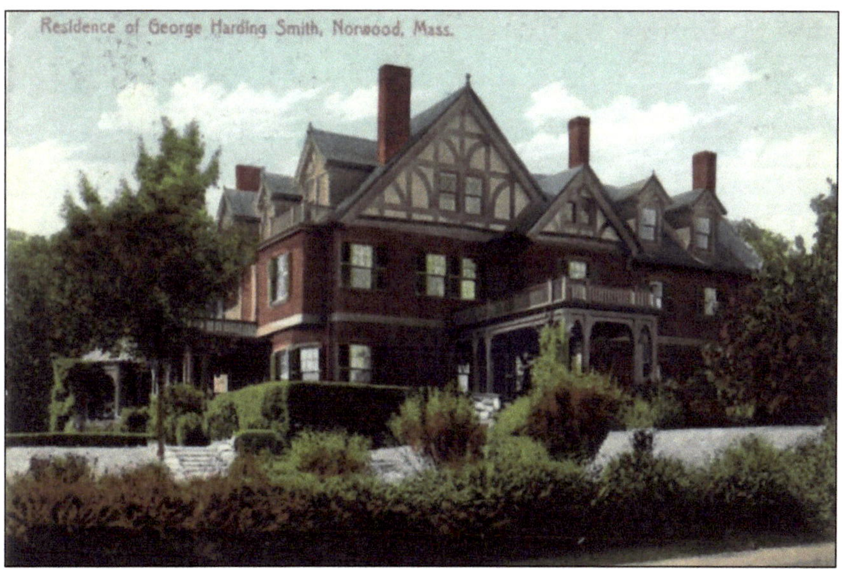

Co-founder of Berwick & Smith, partners in the Norwood Press, George Harding Smith built this stately home on Saunders Road near the J. Stearns Cushing estate. In 1740, it was the site of Ebenezer Everett's home; much altered today, it is an assisted living facility.

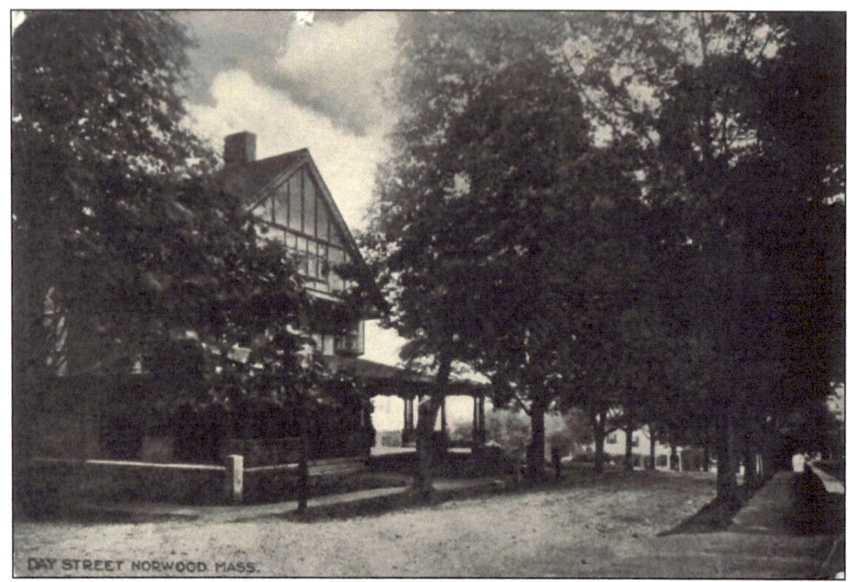

This distinctive home on Day Street was the residence of Lewis and Anna Smith Day and their son, Fred Holland Day. A traditional Victorian mansion with a mansard roof when it was constructed around 1859, the house was transformed between 1890 and 1893.

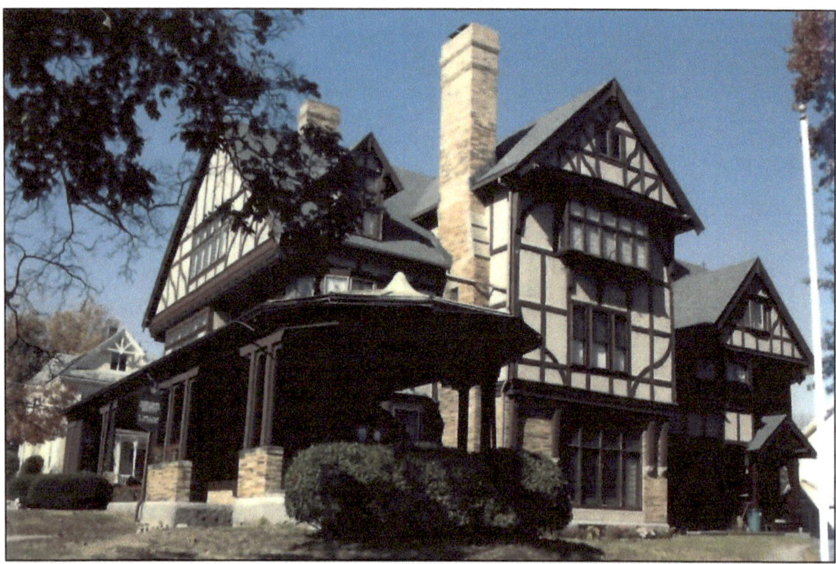

Still standing today, the Day family's three-story Tudoresque showplace is on the National Register of Historic Places. After the death of noted publisher and photographer Fred Holland Day in 1933, it became the headquarters of the Norwood Historical Society.

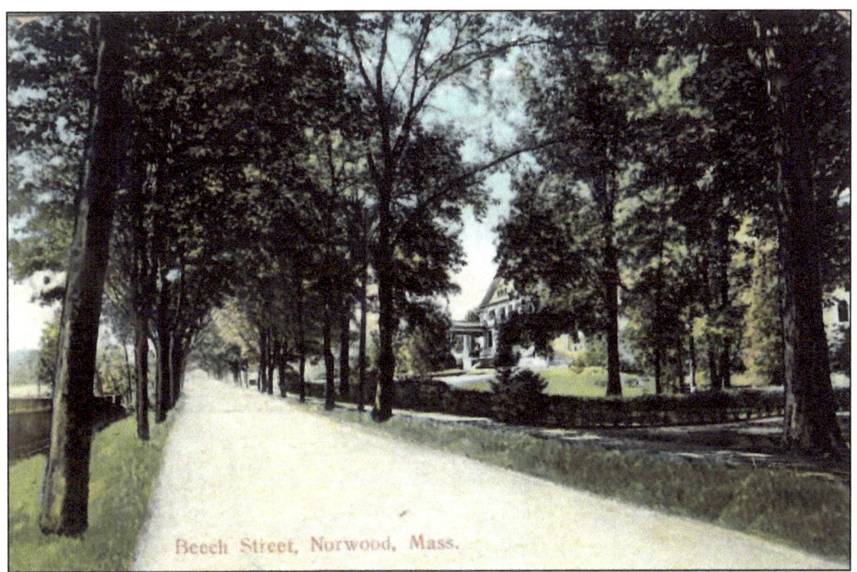

Distributed by E. C. Hunt in his store, this postcard captures the bucolic tree-lined avenues that dominated Norwood into the 1910s. This Beech Street view provides only a glimpse of the mansion of Walter F. Tilton, a prosperous milliner and banker. It was built around 1901.

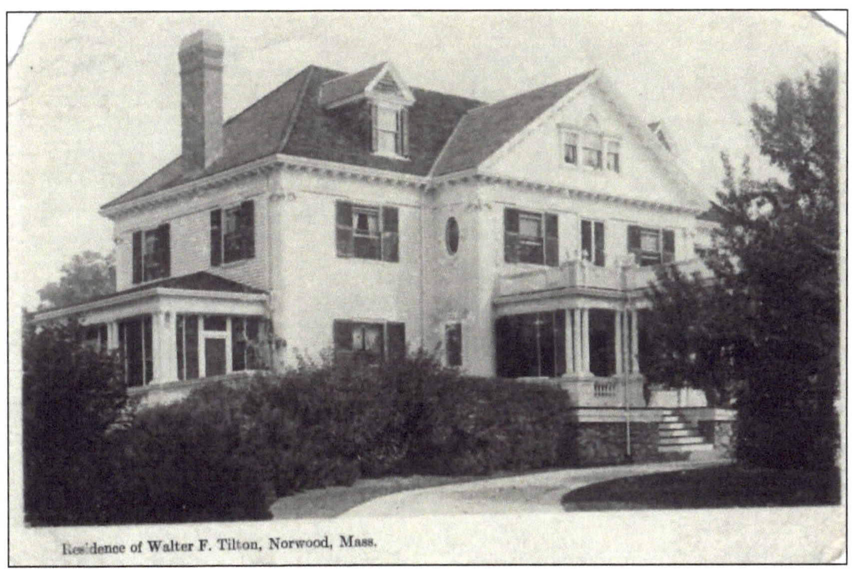

Walter F. Tilton was one of the founders of Norwood Hospital and president of the Norwood Trust Company. He is remembered for his gift to the town of the fifty-bell carillon housed within the municipal building's tower. The mansion still stands today.

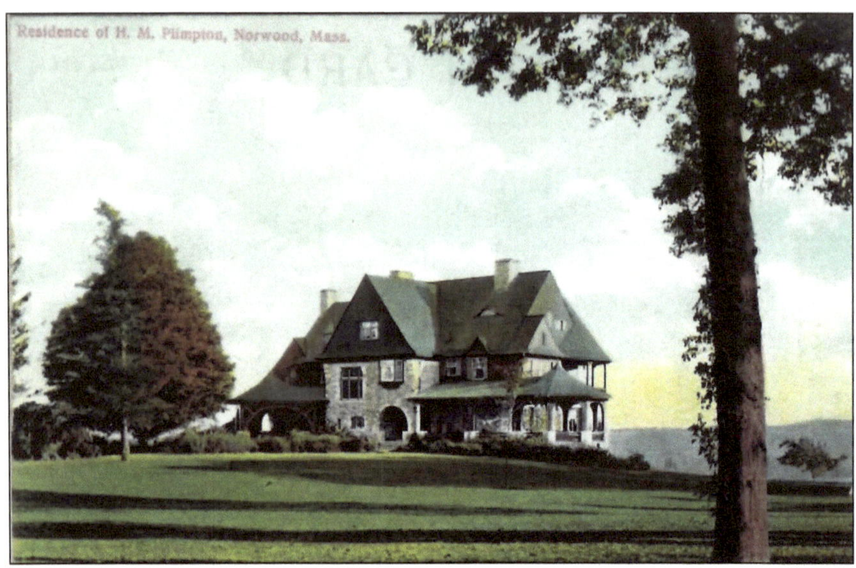

One of two mansions belonging to the Plimpton Press family located in the Chapel Street neighborhood across from Winslow Park (now DAV Park), this magnificent home subsequently became the property of the Veterans of Foreign Wars. It was destroyed by fire in 1957.

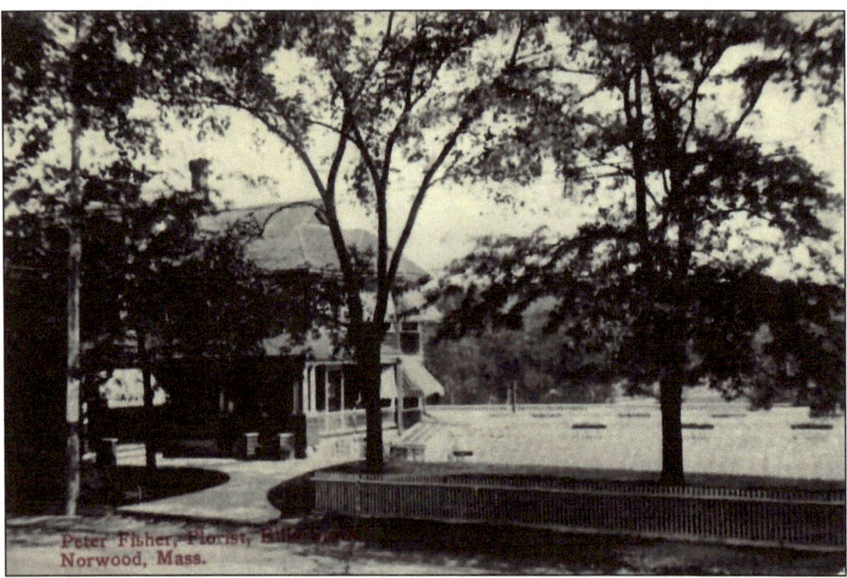

Beginning around 1900, the Fisher family ran a nursery on Washington Street, near Ellis Station, at the northern end of town. The house and business were owned by Peter Fisher when this postcard was printed. Today the property is the site of a condominium complex.

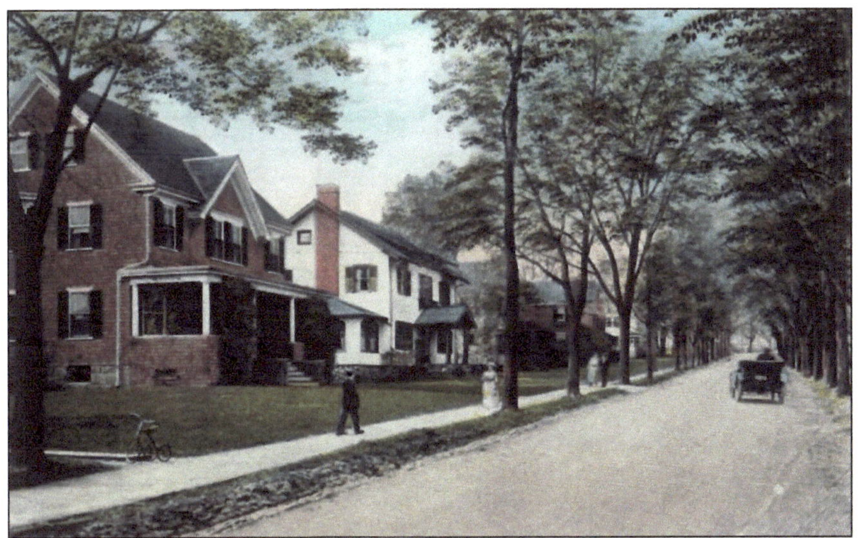

Looking west between Walpole and Washington Streets, this residential section of Winter Street was divided into lots and built out by the early 1900s. During that decade, groups of houses, built on small, manageable lots rather than expansive property like the Shattuck, Morrill, and Plimpton homes, began to appear throughout town. Local residents Milton Howard and Forrest Douglass were the most popular builders. Today, despite the loss of these old-growth trees, this well-maintained Winter Street neighborhood remains distinctive.

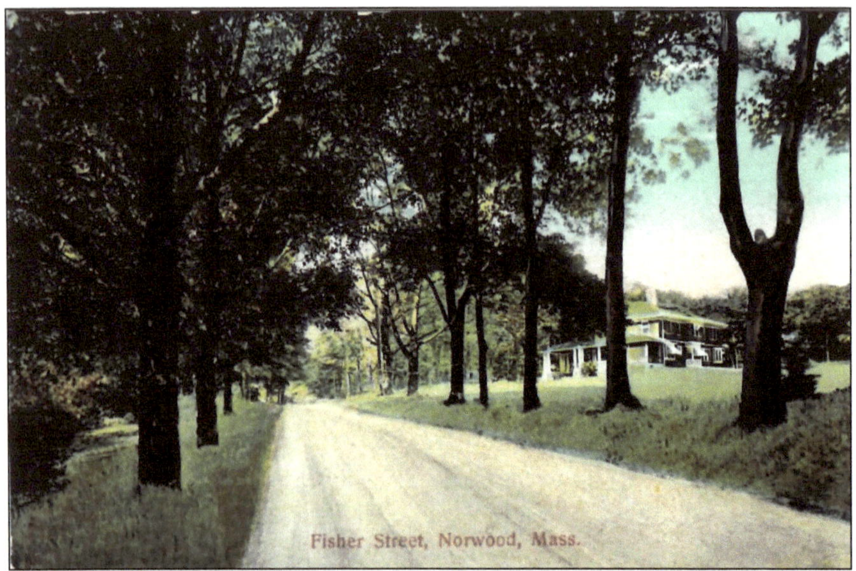

Frank G. Allen built this Shingle-style home on the more rural Fisher Street, near the junction of Chapel and Walpole Streets around 1909. By the time Allen became the Governor of Massachusetts, he had moved into the F. O. Winslow mansion on Walpole Street.

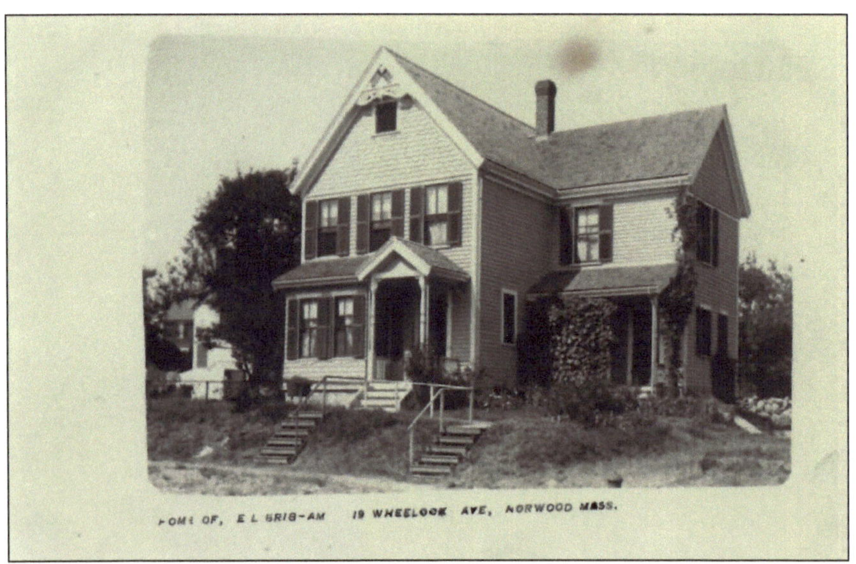

The home of Edmund L. Brigham stood at 19 Wheelock Avenue. Brigham worked at the New York, New Haven and Hartford Railroad Repair Shops on Lenox Avenue. Indicative of the changing occupational times, by the 1930s, it was the home of Richard Finbow, a bookbinder.

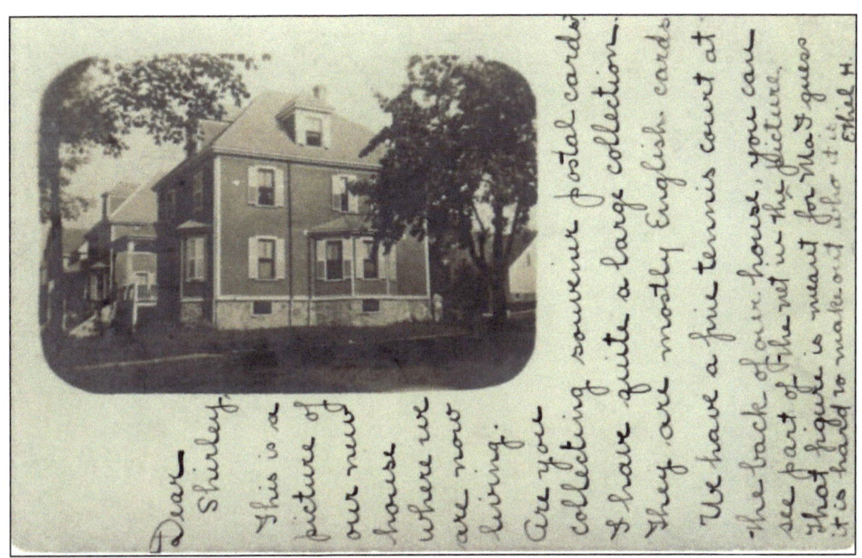

Because messages were not allowed on the address side of postcards c. 1905, this correspondent used the available postcard space to describe her new home in Norwood. It is a handsome, substantial house with, she writes, "a fine tennis court at the back."

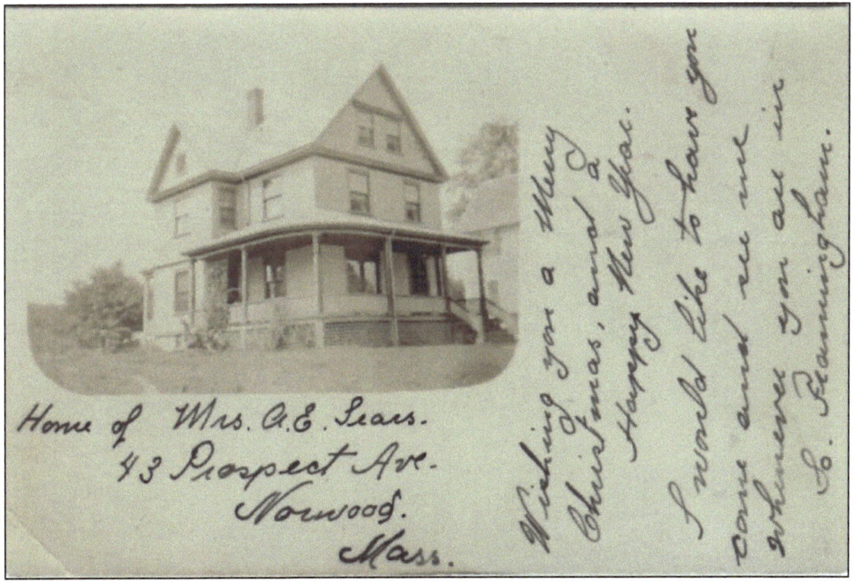

Mrs. Mary Sears used the front of this postcard to send holiday greetings to a friend. She also identifies herself and her home at 43 Prospect Avenue. Sears' husband, Oscar, and son, Russell, were roofers who ran their business from this house as well.

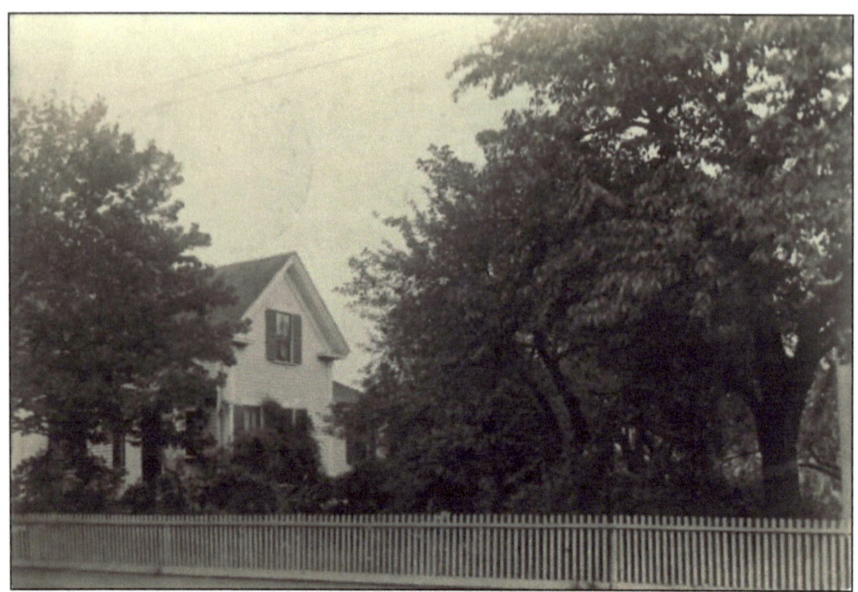

The family living in this house on Linden Street took in lodgers in the early part of the twentieth century. Homes were demolished when the entire street was later taken over by the Norwood Hospital.

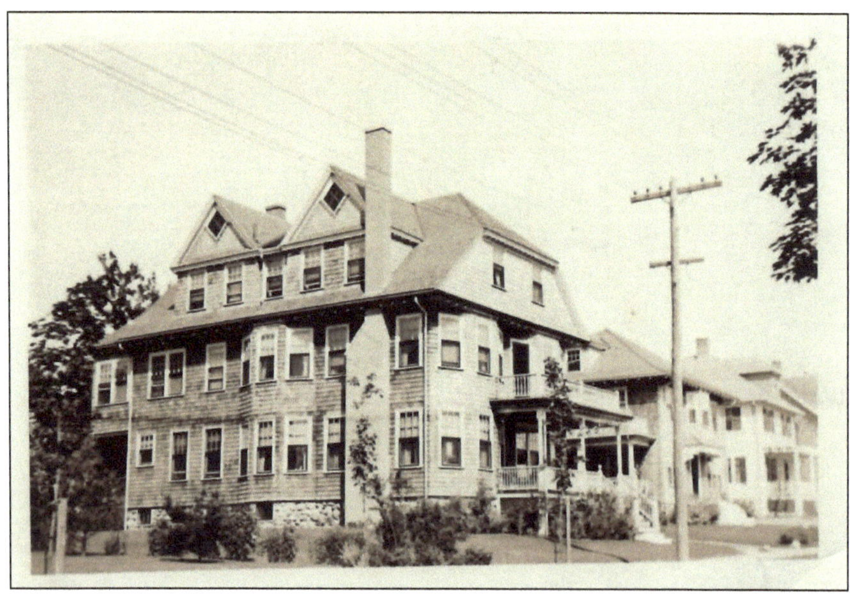

An option to homeownership, boardinghouses proliferated in Norwood in the early part of the twentieth century. By 1918, this house, then owned by Walter Lowell, at 16 Rosemary Street was home to several boarders. Still referred to as "The Rosemary," it continues to be a boarding house today.

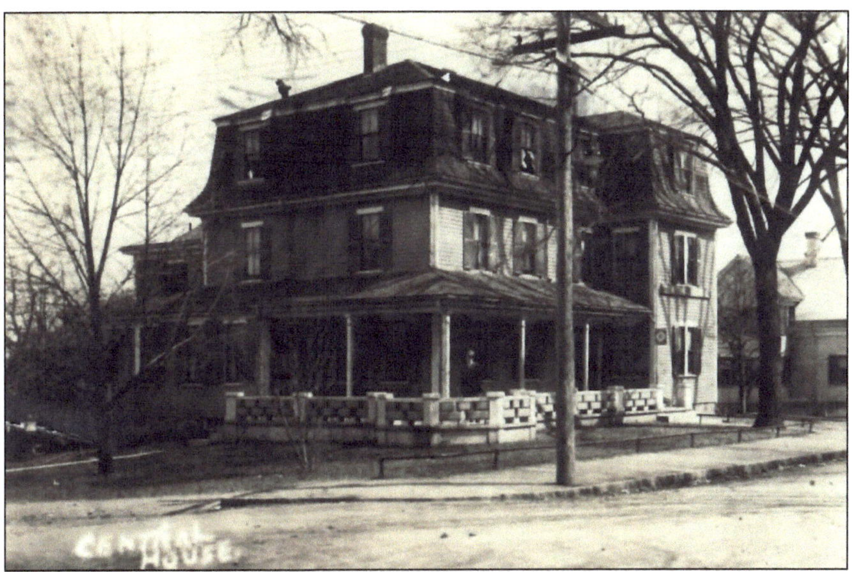

In 1911, the "Central House" at 32 Guild Street was under new management. At that time, George O. Davis, its proprietor, advertised that this boarding house had been "renovated from top to bottom and newly furnished."

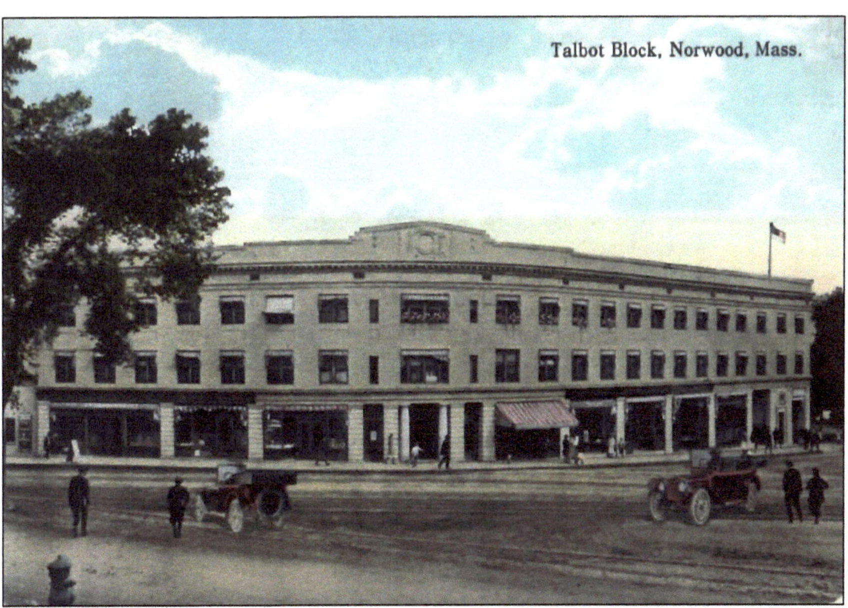

Still standing at the southern end of the central business district today, the Talbot Block, with its distinctive curved façade, was built in 1911. The first structure in Norwood to contain small apartments, it quickly filled. The street-level storefronts continue to thrive with a variety of businesses.

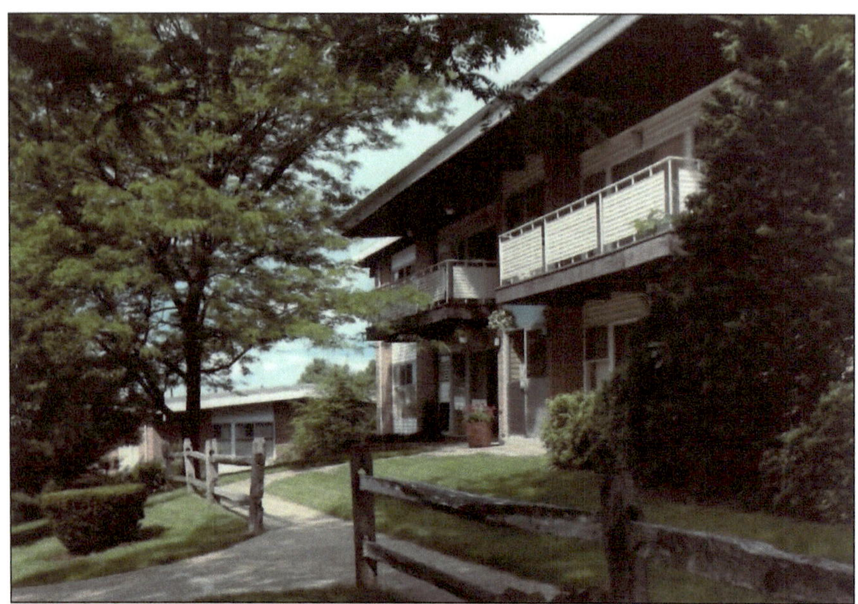

The first complex of its kind to be built in Norwood, the "planned domestic environment" of Windsor Gardens offered one-, two-, and three-bedroom apartments, two- and three-bedroom town houses, a swimming pool, tennis courts, and a commuter rail stop to its residents. The first units opened in 1963. In 1972, historian Bryant Tolles wrote that this complex "suggests the future direction of Norwood's residential growth away from the one-family house or small apartment toward mass habitation." Tolles saw this type of housing as the only way for the town to increase its population.

Five

HOUSES OF WORSHIP

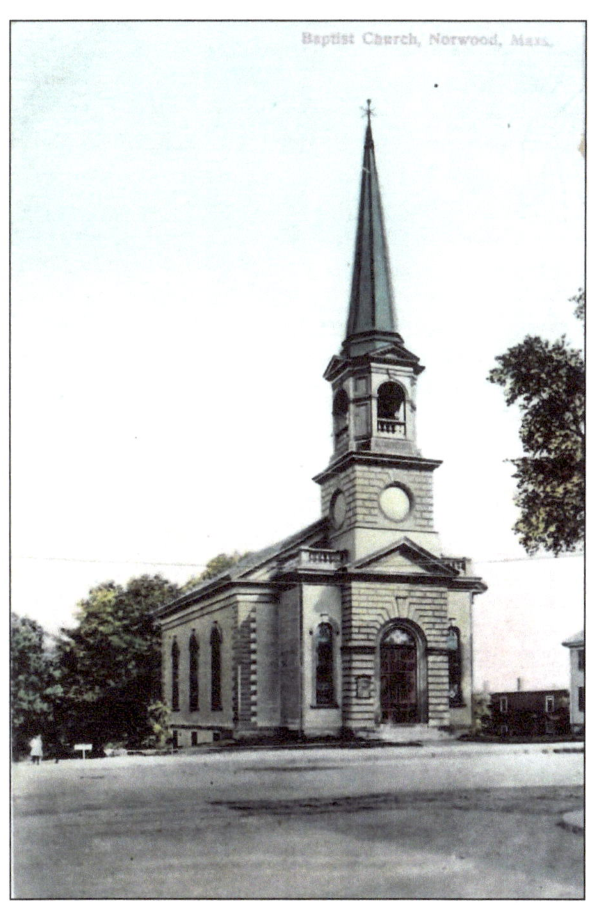

The First Baptist Church was dedicated in 1859. Located in the center of the village's commercial district, the building suffered severe damage during the hurricane of 1938. It was razed in 1950 when the congregation moved to a newly constructed brick building at the corner of Bond and Walpole Streets.

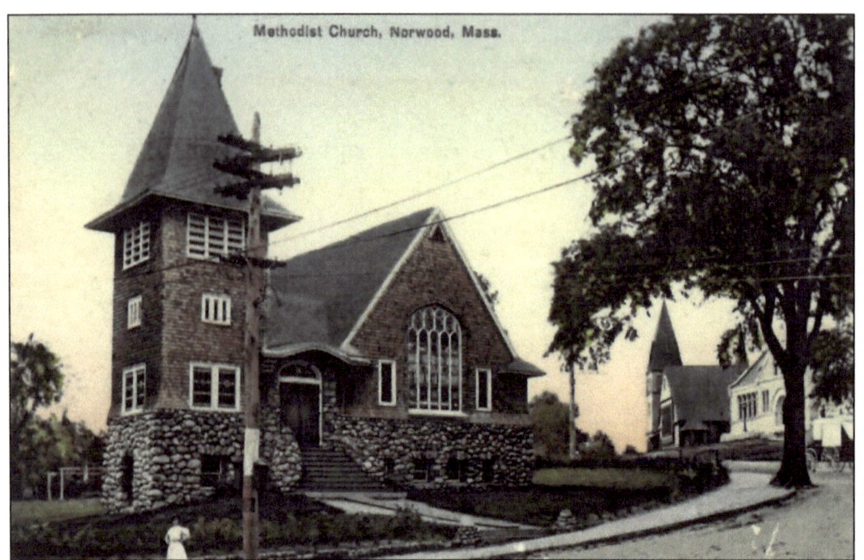

Organized in 1887, this Methodist Episcopal Church at the intersection of Walpole and Washington Streets opened in 1900. In 1934, the Methodists merged with the Universalist congregation to become the United Church. In 1940, this building became the property of the First Church of Christ, Scientist, Norwood.

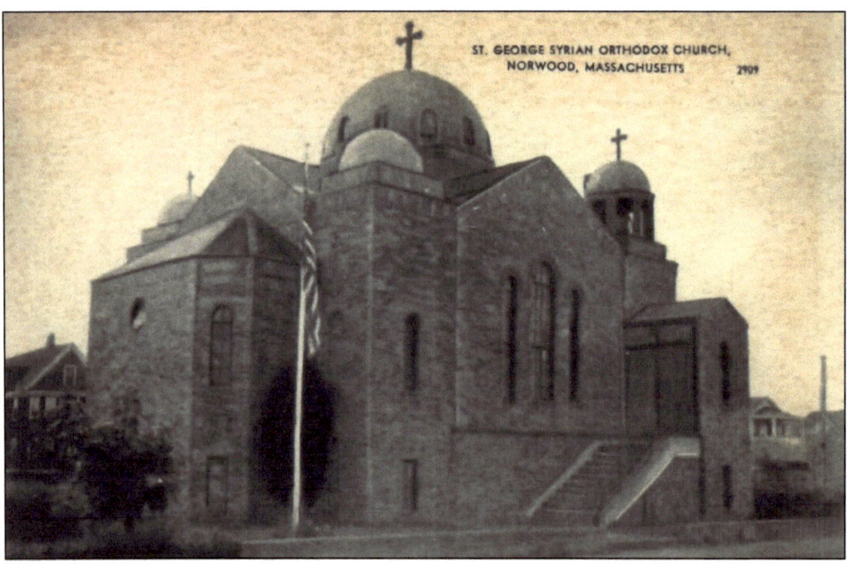

St. George Syrian Orthodox Church was raised on Atwood Avenue in 1921. After a disastrous fire destroyed the church in 1933, this remarkable domed Byzantine Neo-Romanesque sanctuary was constructed on the same site.

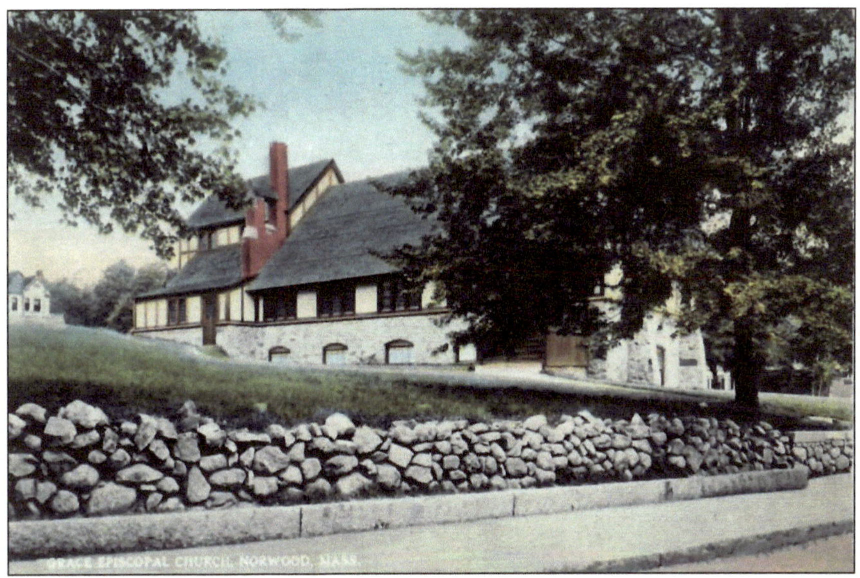

Overlooking Guild Square, the First Grace Church was built in 1910, but ledge rock on the site prevented the original plans from being completed. Subsequently, in 1962, the Grace Episcopal congregation constructed a new church on more spacious grounds on Chapel Street.

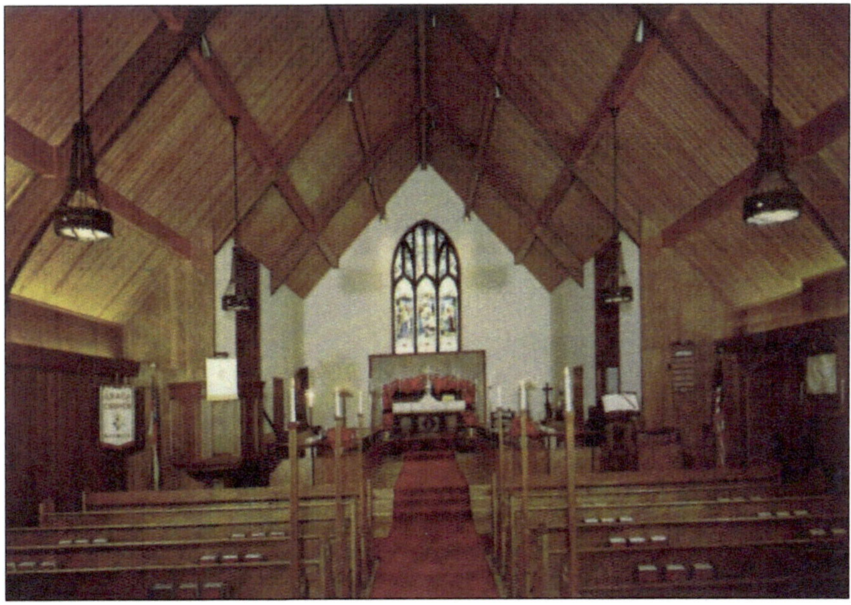

This postcard was distributed before the first Grace Episcopal Church was dismantled. It captures the serenity and spirituality of the building's interior, highlighted by its wooden pews and vaulted ceiling.

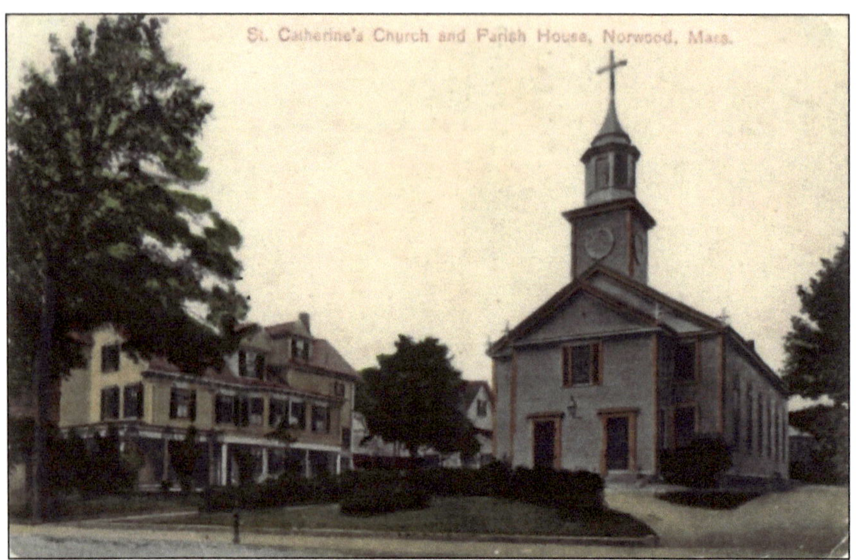

This building was dedicated to St. Catherine of Siena in August of 1863. It was the first church building belonging to Roman Catholics in South Dedham. Originally the home of the Universalist Society, the building was sold to the Catholic congregation for $3,300.

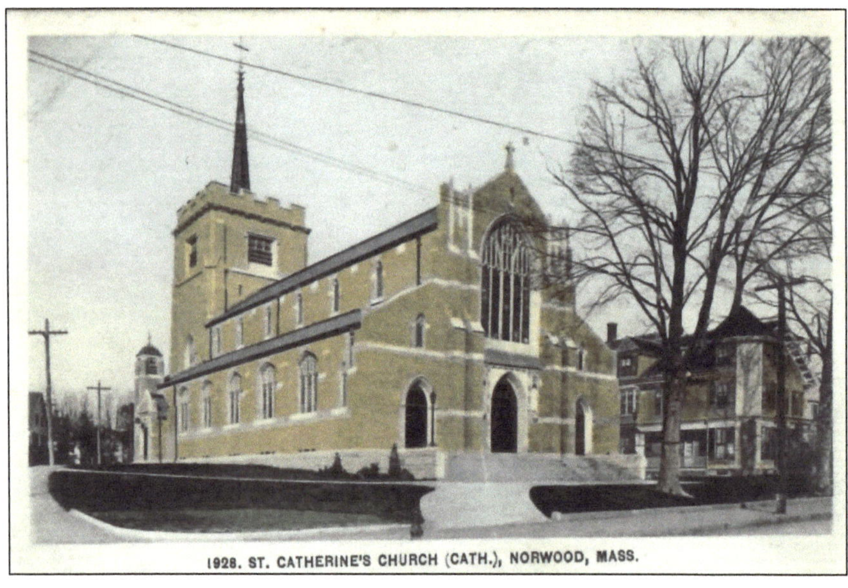

Built between 1908 and 1910, and designed by ecclesiastical architects Maginnis and Walsh, St. Catherine of Siena Roman Catholic Church remains a landmark at the corner of Nahatan and Washington Streets. The rectory to the right of the building was later replaced.

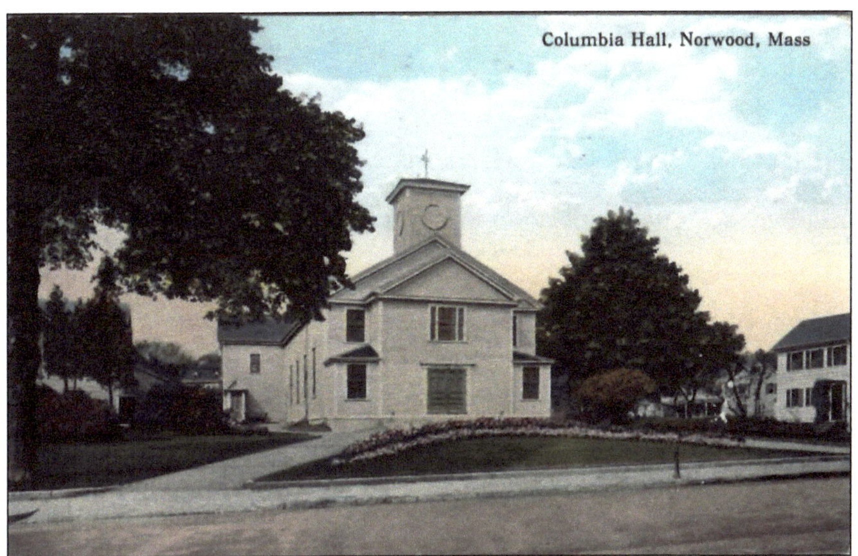

After the opening of the new St. Catherine of Siena Church, this structure, renamed "Columbia Hall," which had once provided services for Universalist and Roman Catholic congregations, became a function and meeting room. It was razed in 1927.

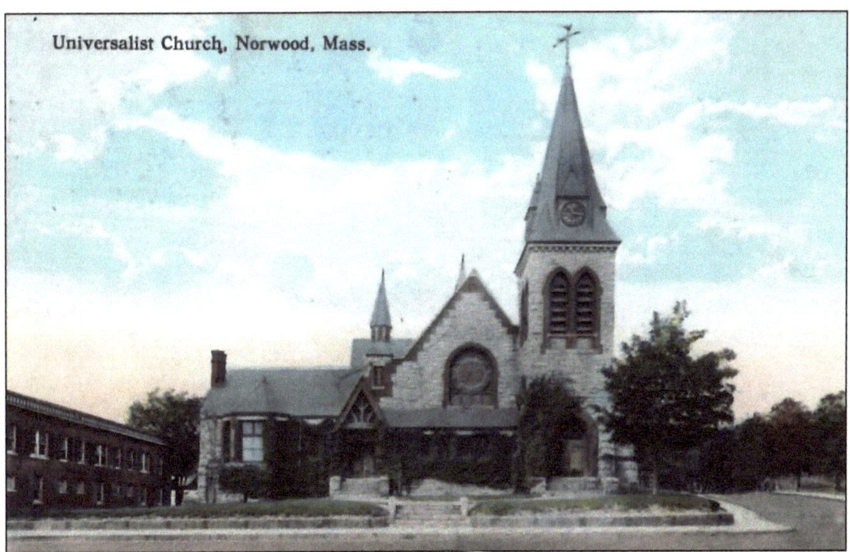

Built in 1885, this impressive Romanesque Revival building replaced a distinctive Neo-Georgian style church, which had served the Universalist congregation for twenty years. That structure had been totally destroyed by a devastating fire. Now the United Church, the building still stands across Nahatan Street from St. Catherine's.

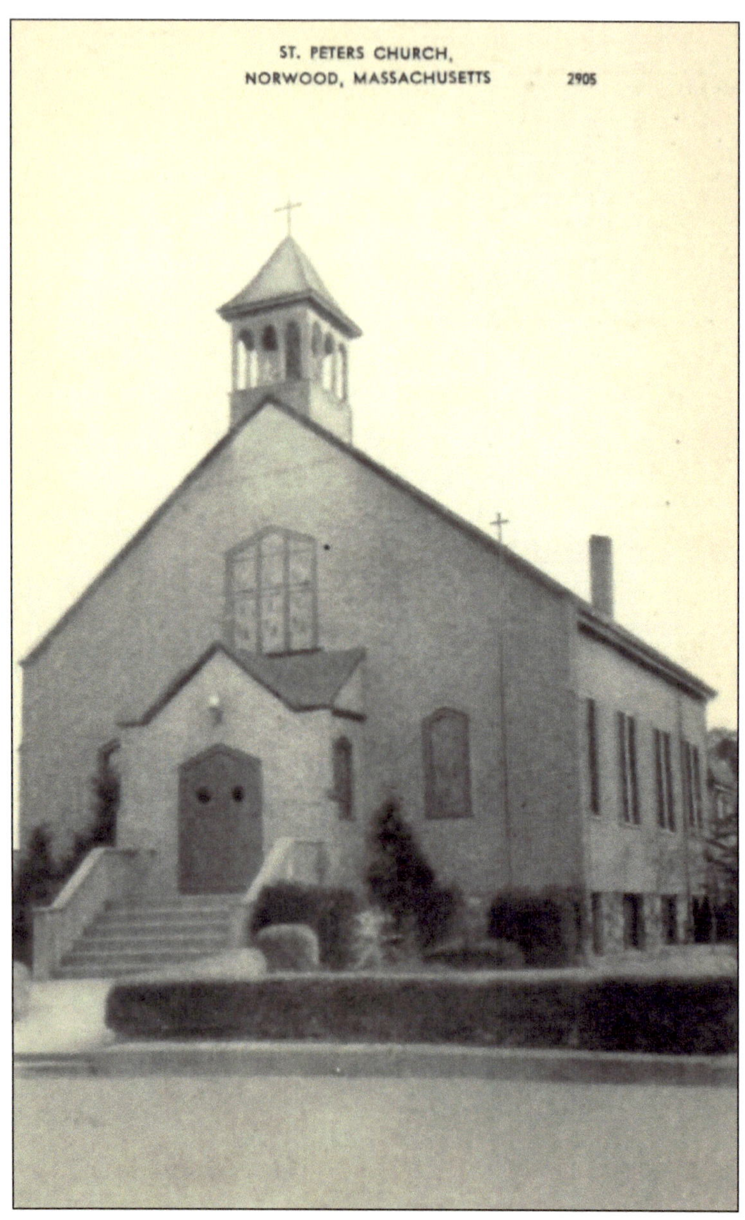

Norwood's Polish Catholics first held services at St. George Lithuanian Church on St. James Avenue. After a few years, however, the Polish congregants established their own parish in 1919 and celebrated their first Mass in St. Peter's Catholic Church on St. Joseph Avenue in 1920. This small congregation continued to thrive until 1997 when it was closed by the Archdiocese of Boston as part of a parish consolidation program. The building was renovated into condominiums.

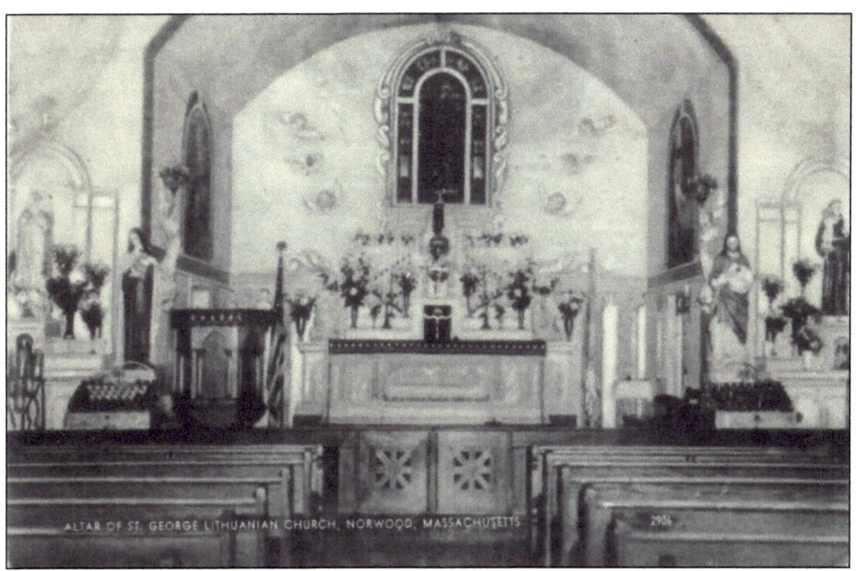

This view of the interior of St. George Lithuanian Church is all that remains of a vibrant community of believers. This Roman Catholic parish, founded in 1915, built their church on St. James Avenue. It too was closed, and the building has become condominiums.

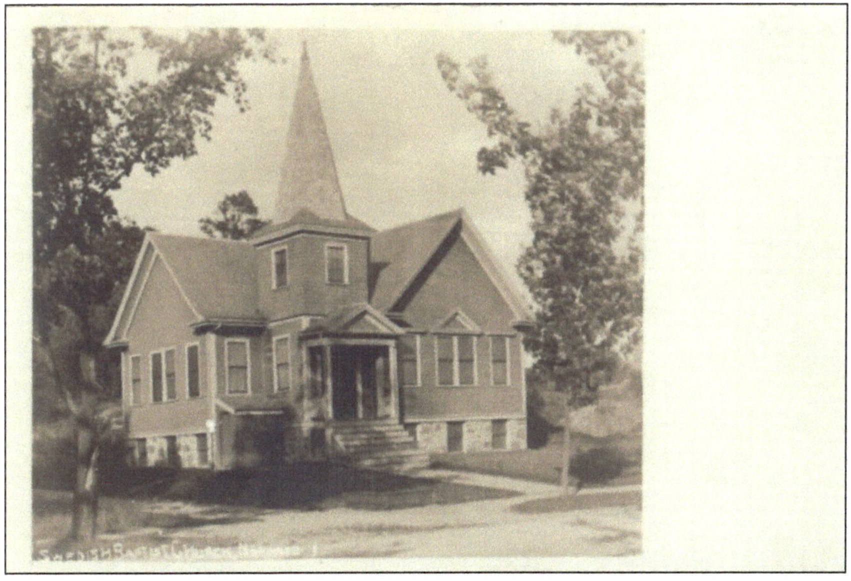

Organized in 1898, the Swedish Baptist congregation of Norwood built this church on Chapel Street, opposite Savin Avenue. In the mid-twentieth century, the sanctuary was moved, renovated, and enlarged. It stands today at the corner of Walpole and Berwick Streets as the Trinity Baptist Church.

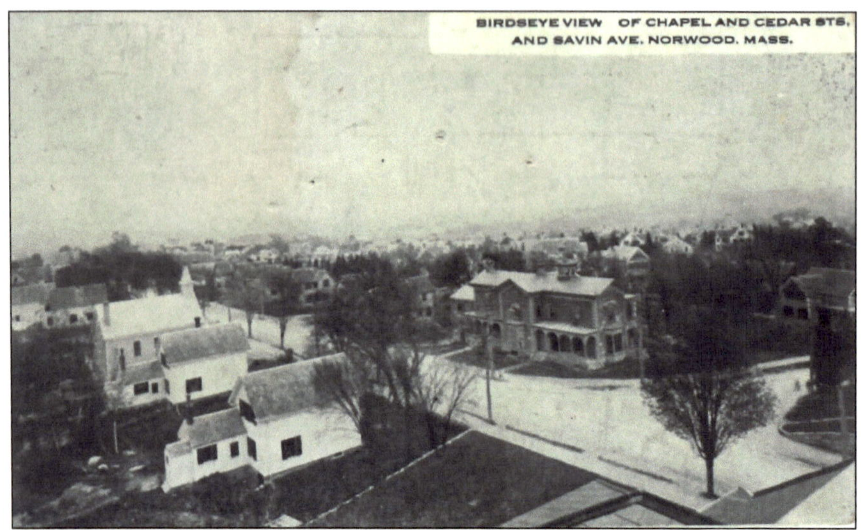

For a time after their arrival in Norwood, Swedish Baptists, Congregationalists, and Lutherans all worshiped together in the large house at the corner of Chapel and Cedar Streets shown here. Eventually, each formed their own parish. The Swedish Congregational Church can be seen to the left.

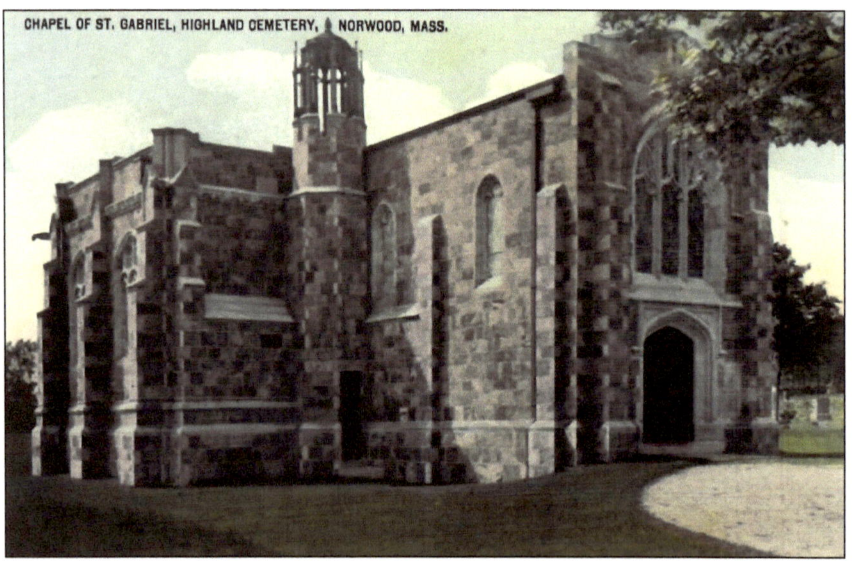

Designed by the famed architectural firm of Cram, Goodhue & Ferguson, the Neo-Gothic Chapel of St. Gabriel the Archangel, which stands in Highland Cemetery, was erected by Lewis and Anna Smith Day in memory of their parents. Consecrated in May 1903, it was donated to the town.

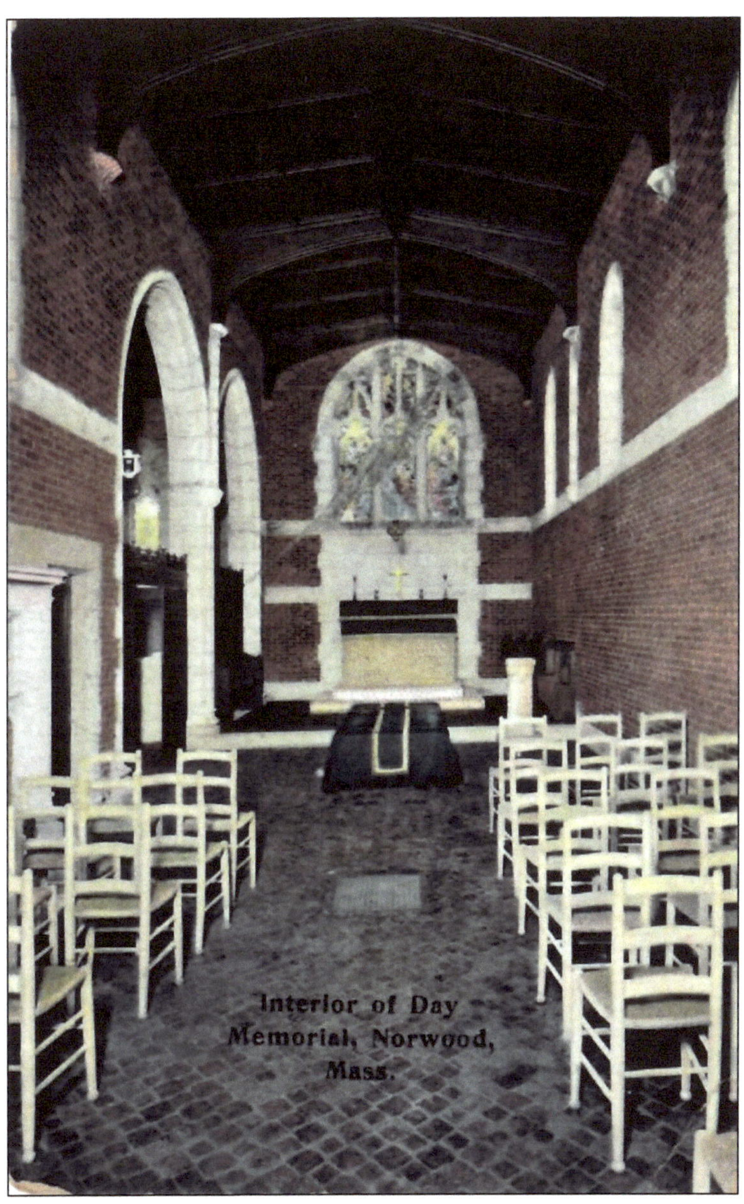

A rather rare mortuary chapel, the interior of the Chapel of St. Gabriel the Archangel at Highland Cemetery has an elegance that relies on its simple proportions rather than any extravagant ornamentation. There is a small altar, bier, and seating. To the left, behind a wrought iron gate is a chamber that holds the tombs of Lewis and Anna Smith Day. Funeral services for any Norwood resident may be held there free-of-charge, irrespective of religious beliefs.

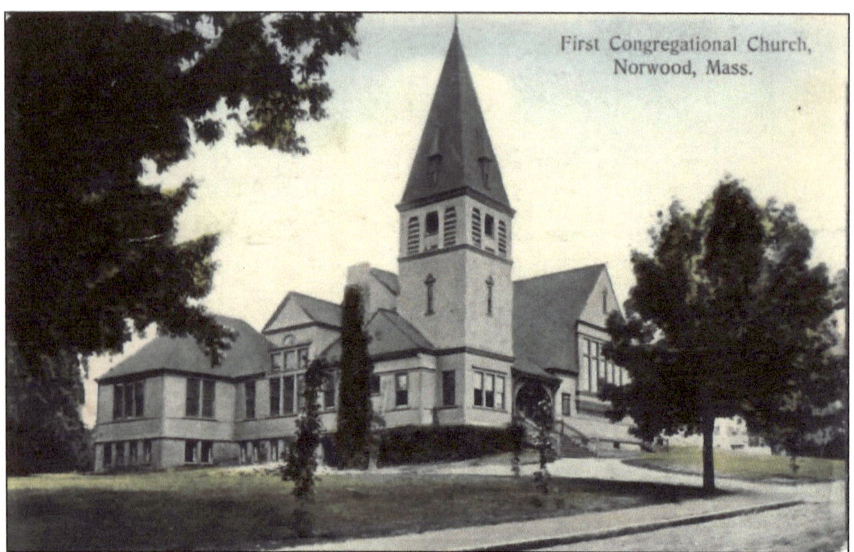

The South Parish of Dedham, now Norwood, was founded in 1736 by members of what today has become the First Congregational Church. The fourth meetinghouse of that congregation was located next to the Morrill Memorial Library at the corner of Winter and Walpole Streets until 1961.

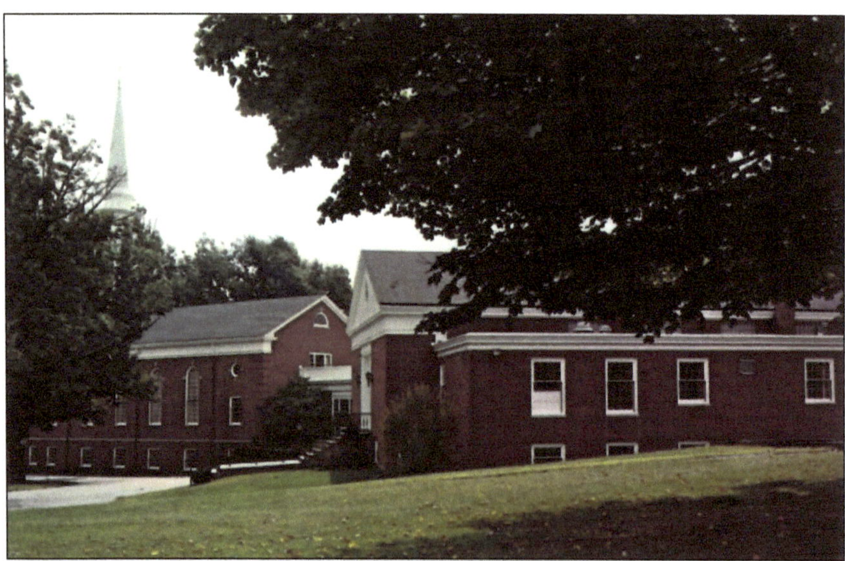

The present, handsome, red-brick, Neo-Federal home of the First Congregational Church was designed by ecclesiastical architect Arland Dirlam. On the corner of Winter and Walpole Streets opposite the fourth meetinghouse (above), the church stands on land that was once the site of the Edmund Shattuck mansion.

Six

PUBLIC BUILDINGS & LANDMARKS

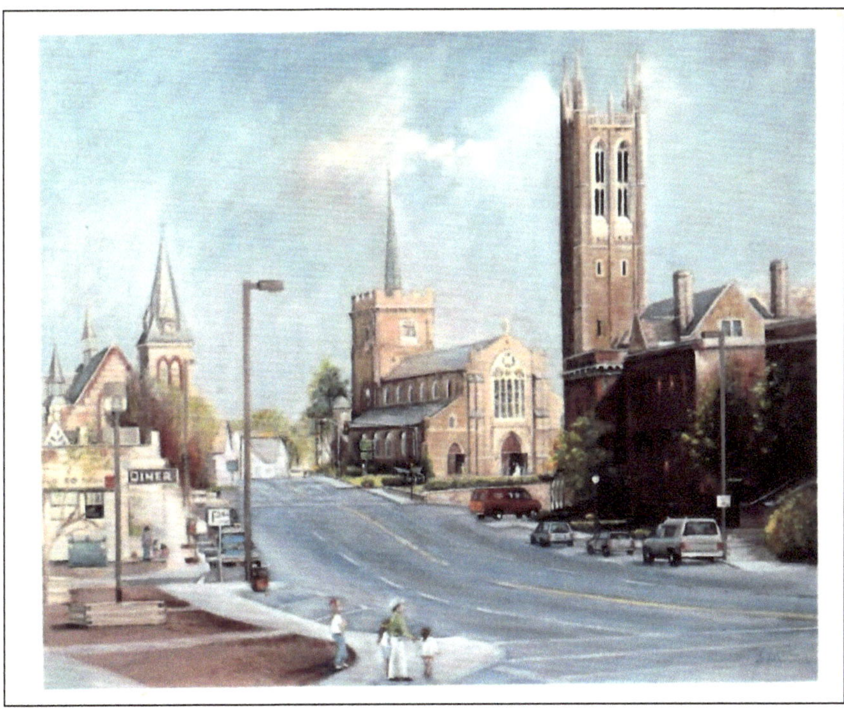

This view looking west on Nahatan Street captures an iconic Norwood scene. The town hall (right), St. Catherine of Siena Church (center) and the Universalist Church (rear left). The Diner (near left) completes this image by Judith Ciardi, made into a postcard in 1995.

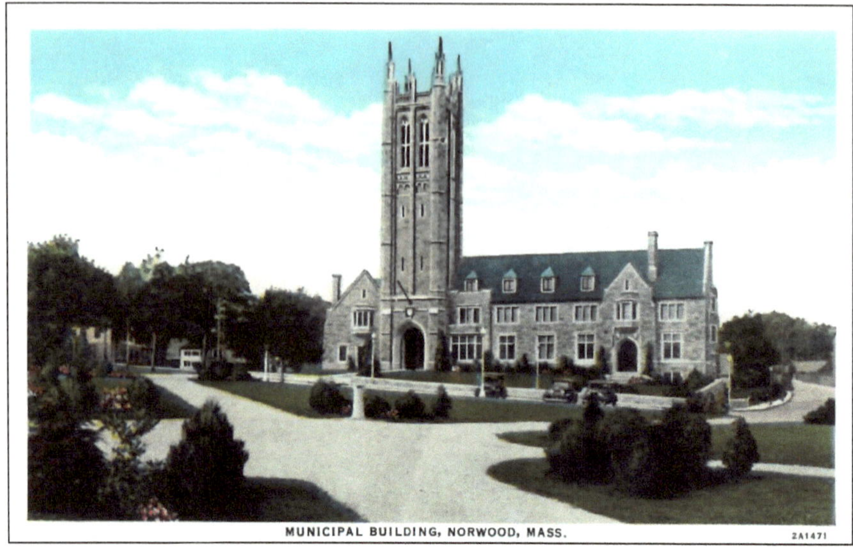

Constructed of Weymouth seam-face granite and featuring a soaring carillon tower, Norwood's Neo-Gothic Memorial Municipal Building was dedicated on November 11, 1928. The building was designed by architect William G. Upham, a Norwood native. The fifty-bell carillon, housed in its tower, was donated by Walter Tilton.

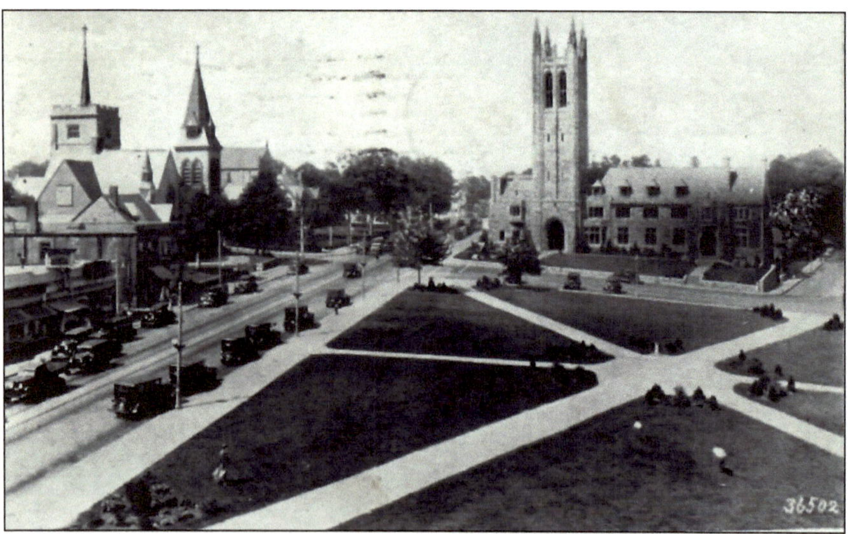

Envisioned as early as 1912, the town square was designed by famed landscape architect Arthur A. Shurtleff. Several older buildings were removed, including the former Tiot Tavern, to create it. Renamed Veterans of Foreign Wars Park after World War II, the common remains the cherished center of the community.

58

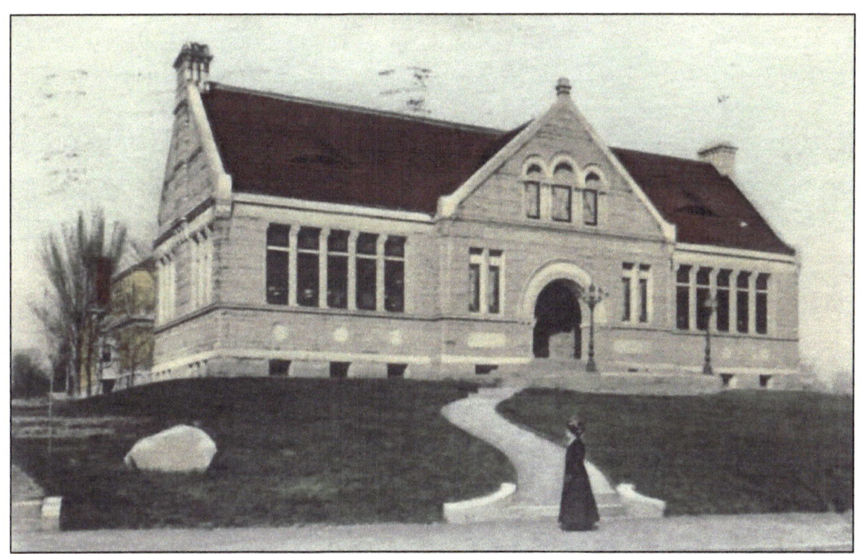

Built by George H. and Louisa Morrill in memory of their daughter, the Sarah Bond Morrill Memorial Library opened in 1898. The Romanesque-Revival-style structure, featuring a red tile roof and eyebrow dormer windows, was Norwood's first stand-alone library building.

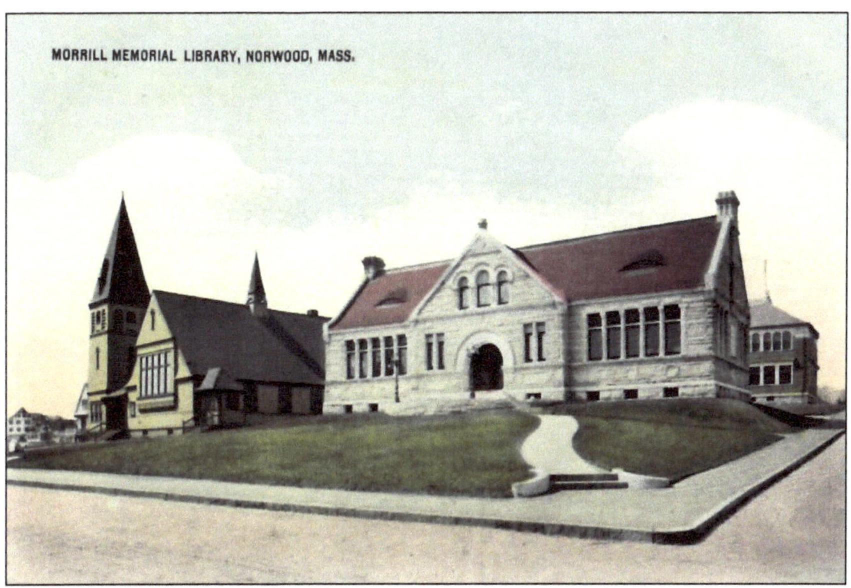

Norwood's first high school, later the Beacon Elementary School, can be seen to the rear of the Morrill Memorial Library. The fourth meetinghouse of the Congregational Church, built in 1884, is on the left. The three buildings made "Beacon Hill" an impressive institutional complex.

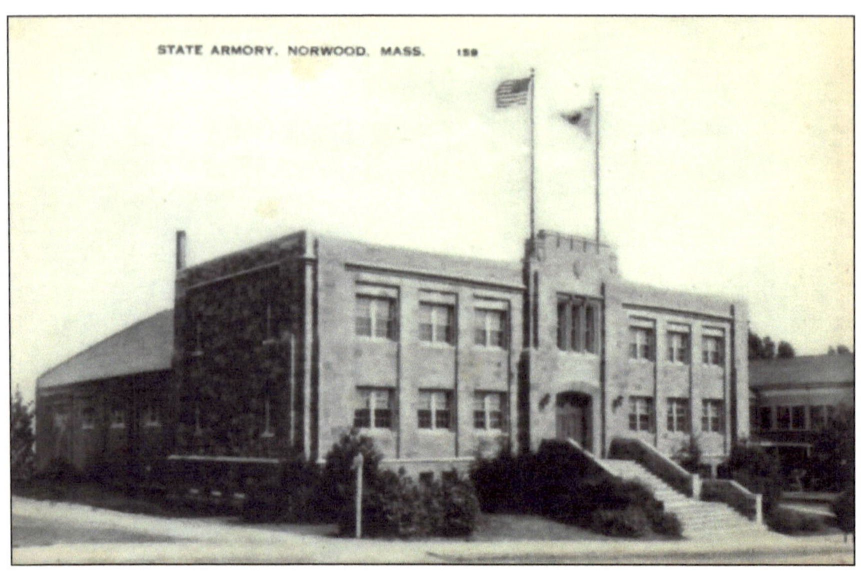

Governor Frank G. Allen advocated for the state to build this State Armory at Norwood. It was dedicated in January of 1930. After it was decommissioned, the Commonwealth of Massachusetts sold the building to the town in 1984. It is currently home to Norwood's Recreation Department.

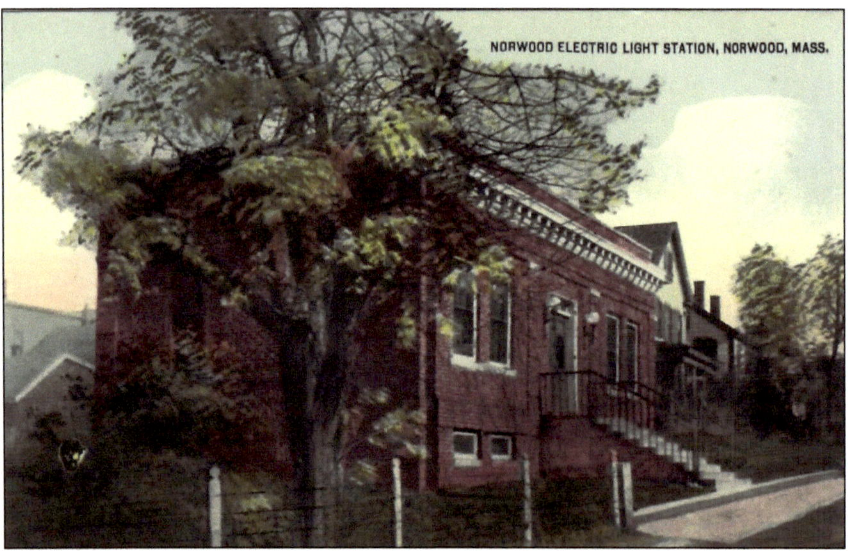

The first Norwood Electric Light Station was established in 1907 in this building on Central Street near the town hall. Although today's Norwood Light Broadband is housed elsewhere, it remains municipally-owned and operated. This building still contains town offices and some essential light department equipment.

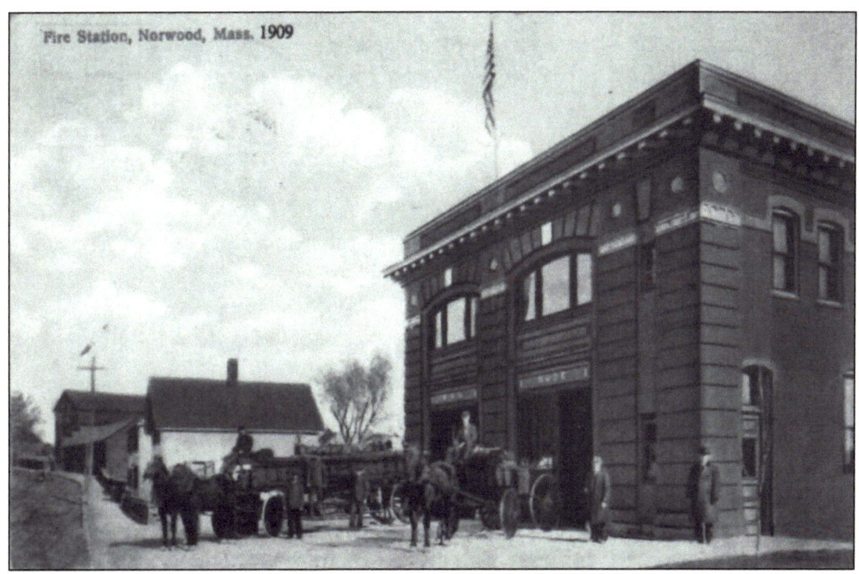

Located at the corner of Nahatan and Central Streets, this two-story brick facility was the second building dedicated to Norwood's fire department. The department had quickly outgrown the hook and ladder and hose house built in 1887. This 1909 image captures the department's horse-drawn wagons.

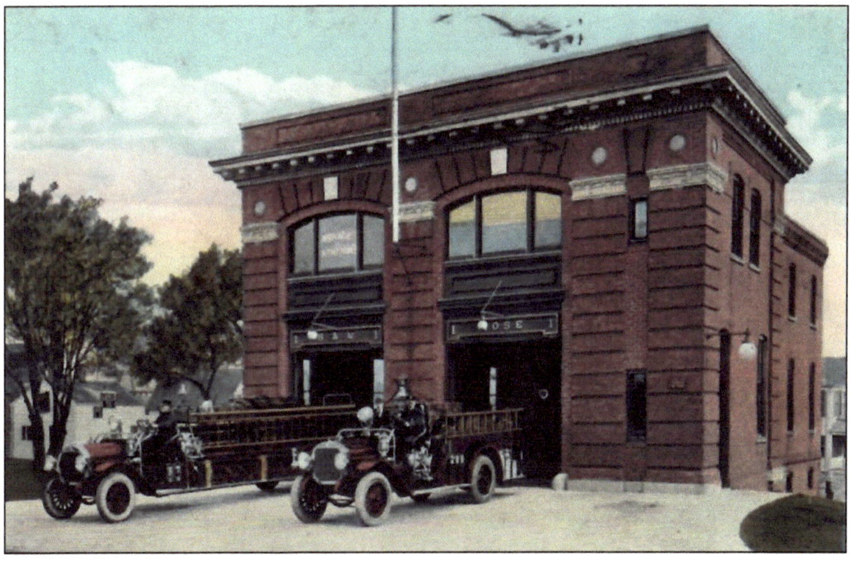

By the time this postcard image of the fire station was published, the fire department boasted modern mechanical engines. And the police department was using the second floor. Although this building remains town-owned, both departments have moved to a larger, more expansive facility.

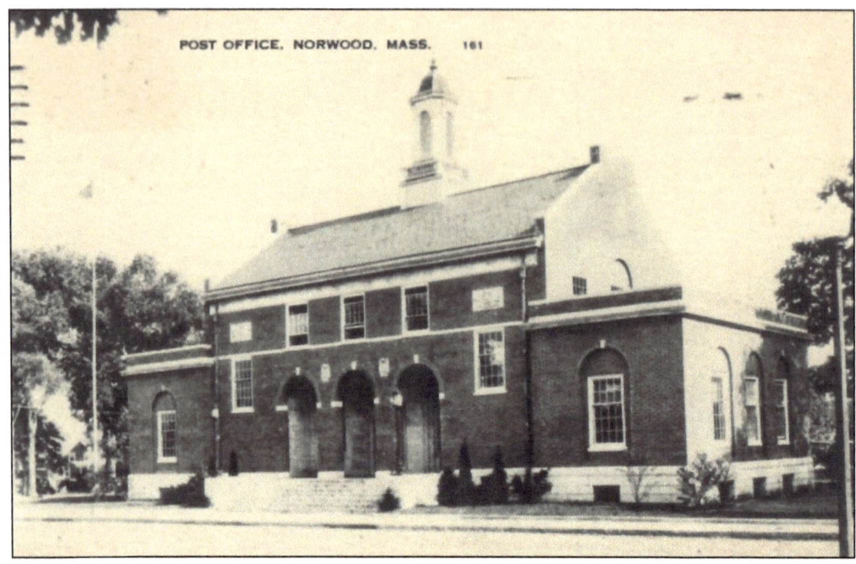

After being housed in various locations, the post office received its own building in 1934 after the Everett School was razed and Central Street extended. Like the town hall, it was designed by William G. Upham. Enlarged in 1965, the facility remains across from Guild Square Park today.

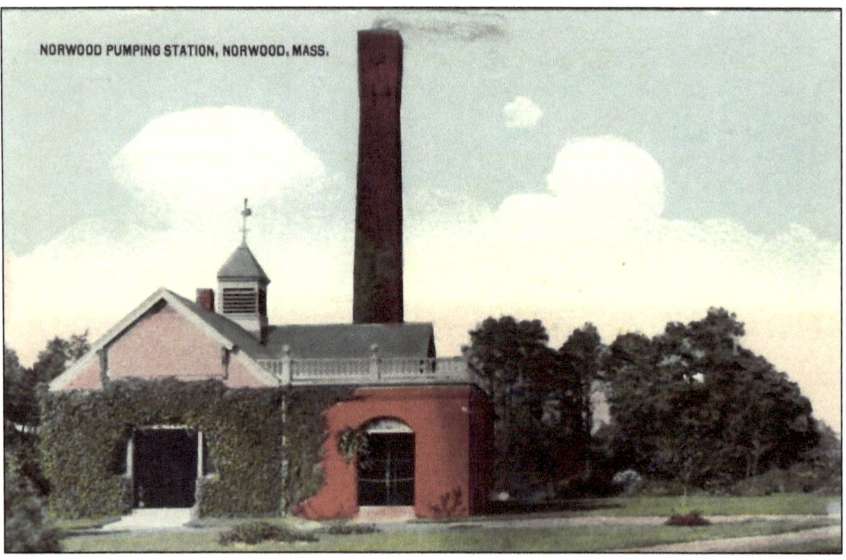

The town acquired Buckmaster Pond around 1880 and constructed this brick pumping station, enlarged in 1904. For some years, the station was Norwood's sole centralized public water source. In 1957, the town joined the Metropolitan Water System (now the MWRA); Buckmaster remains a potential auxiliary water source.

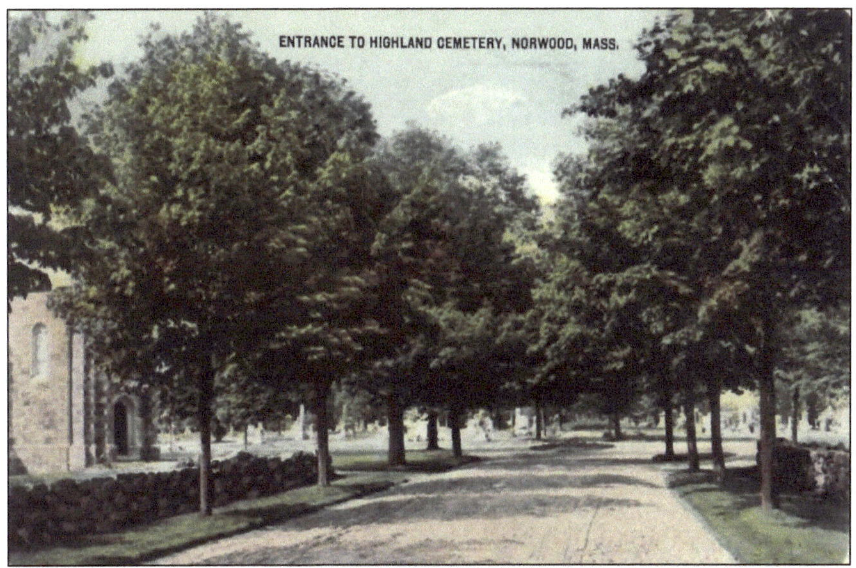

Shortly after Norwood was incorporated, officials recognized the need for a new burial ground since the Old Cemetery on Washington Street was near capacity. Founded in 1880, Highland Cemetery on Winter Street today has both an administration building and a chapel at the crest of this entryway.

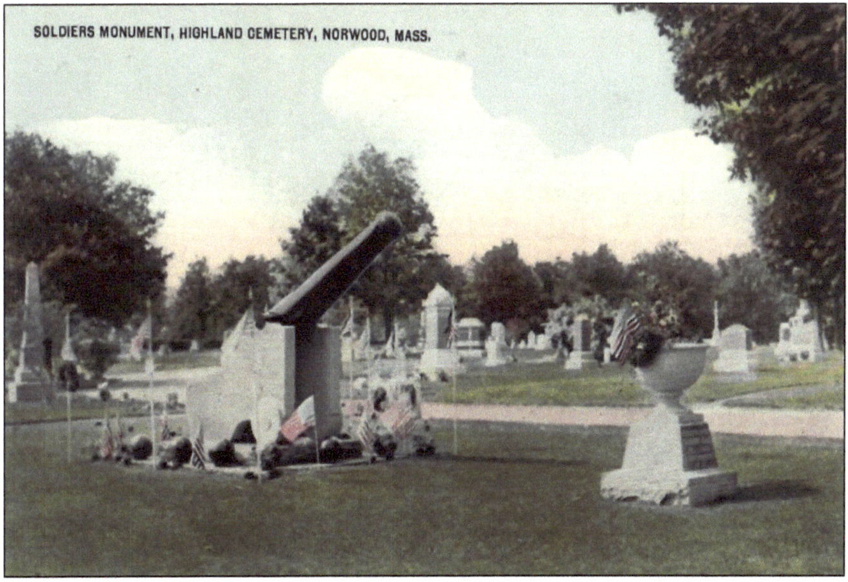

Near St. Gabriel's Chapel in Highland Cemetery stands a cannon dedicated by the George K. Bird Grand Army of the Republic Post 169 in memory of comrades who lost their lives in the Civil War. Nearby is a memorial to the Unknown Dead of that same conflict.

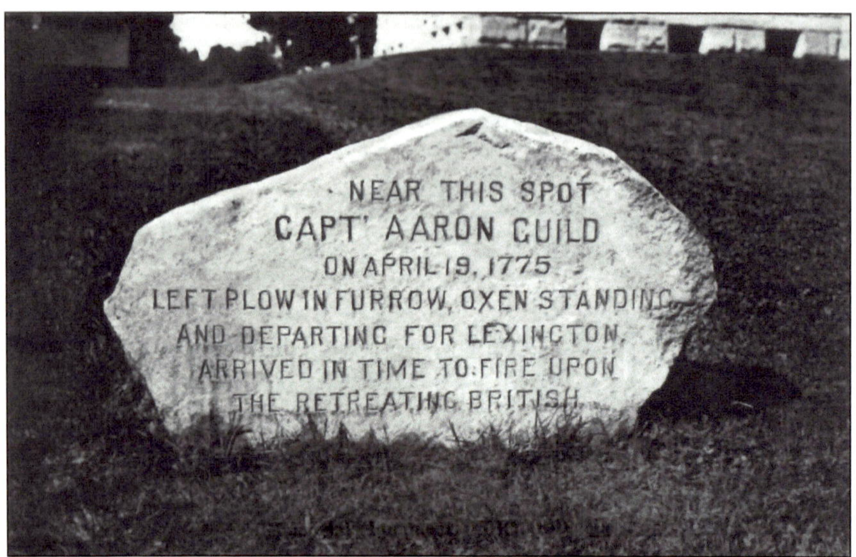

In 1902, Norwood celebrated its first Old-Home Week and dedicated a stone to Capt. Aaron Guild as a representative of all the South Dedham militia men of April 19, 1775. Despite the inscription, Guild and others actually mustered in Dedham, not Lexington. The stone still stands in front of the library.

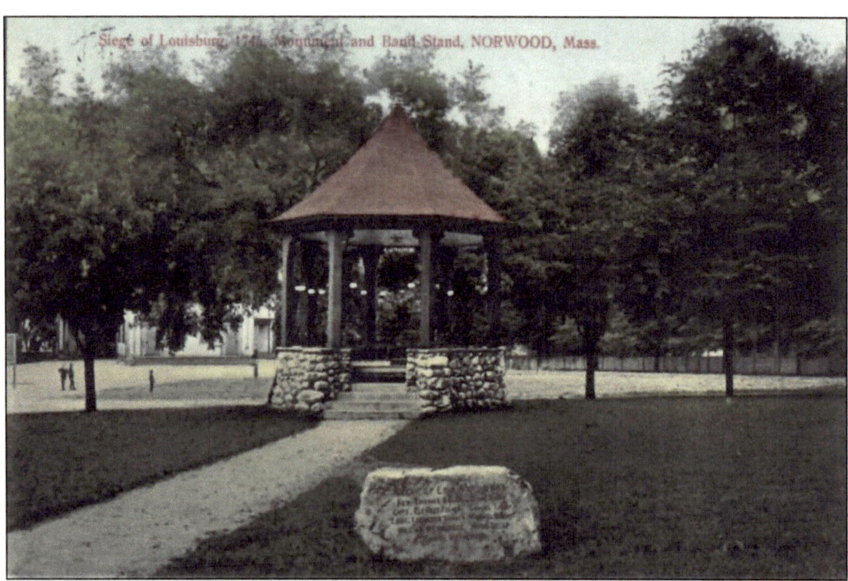

The unveiling of the Siege of Louisburg commemorative stone was held on July 23, 1903. Engraved with the names of the nine men from South Dedham who participated in that 1745 military action, the stone is seen here in front of the bandstand at Guild Square Park.

Seven

LEISURE

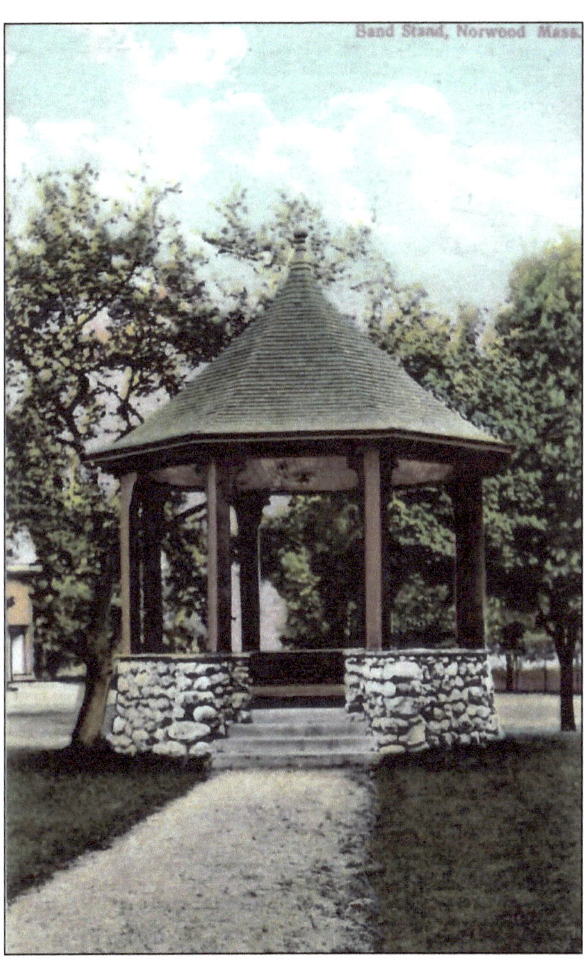

Due to the haphazard nature of the development in South Dedham, later Norwood, there were few parks for leisure activity. By 1903, however, thanks to the efforts of James Berwick of Norwood Press, a bandstand was built at Guild Square. It became the gathering spot for community activities.

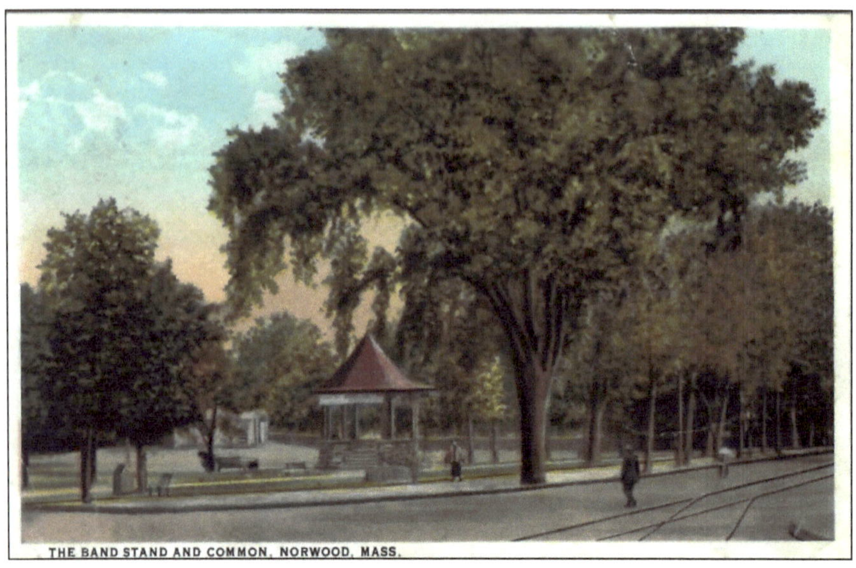

A tree-encased setting surrounded by the Guild and Everett Schools, the Central House, and the Methodist Church, Guild Square Park was developed on land once owned by Moses Guild. It was the site of a freight wagon barn, a factory, and a tenement before it became a park.

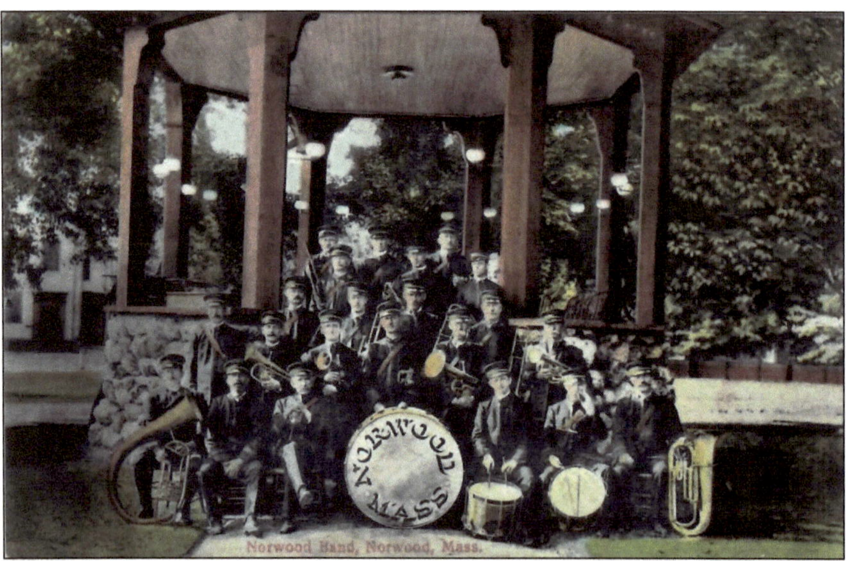

The South Dedham Musical Association was founded in 1866. After Norwood's incorporation, it became the Norwood Brass Band. The band earned a solid reputation in Norfolk County and beyond and offered a popular series of summer evening concerts at the bandstand which was finally demolished in 1955.

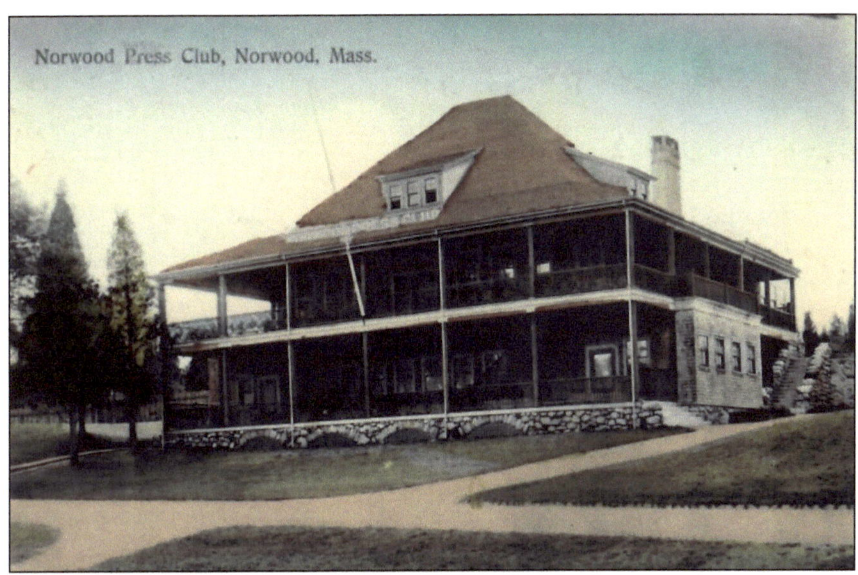

In 1907, the Norwood Press Club, organized for the employees of the Norwood Press, opened on property adjacent to the Winslow School. It quickly became a popular social and recreational facility. Athletic contests, company picnics, and even ice skating in the winter months were held there.

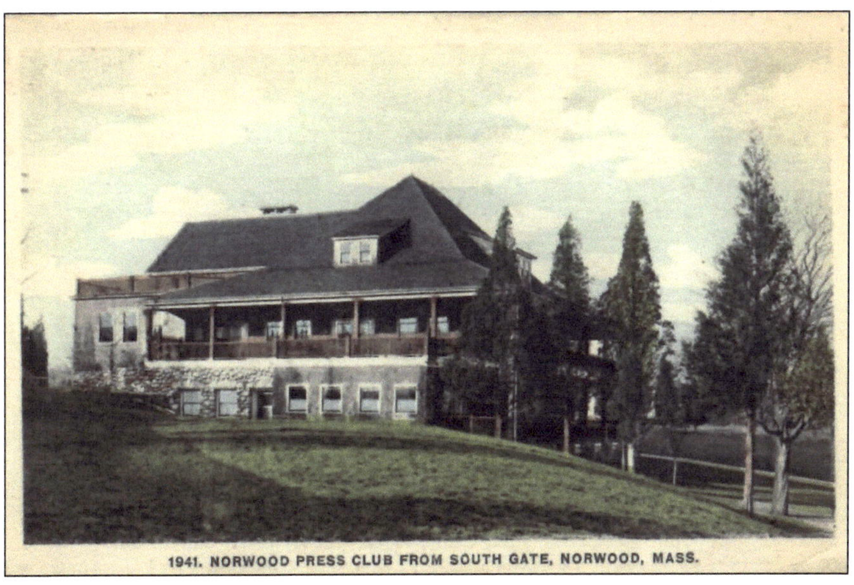

The Norwood Press Club was a haven for Press employees and their families until 1923 when the building was acquired by the Norwood Lodge of the Benevolent and Protective Order of Elks. Extensively renovated, the property is skill known as "Elks Park" today.

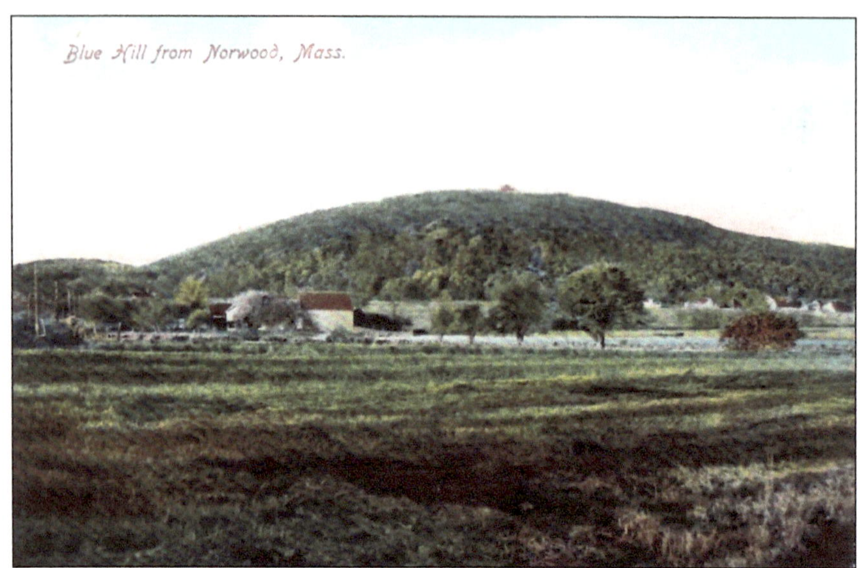

Great Blue Hill got its name because of its blueish color and is a notable landmass even viewed from Norwood. Its summit is the highest point in Greater Boston. Because of this, Abbot Lawrence Rotch placed a meteorological observatory on the site in 1885. In 1893, influenced by pioneer landscape architect Charles Eliot, the Metropolitan Parks Commission purchased thousands of acres, including Blue Hill, and set the land aside for public recreation. Even today, its trails are a destination for nature-loving Norwood residents and Eliot Tower provides a stunning view of the city of Boston and surrounding hills. In the winter, a ski slope is equally popular.

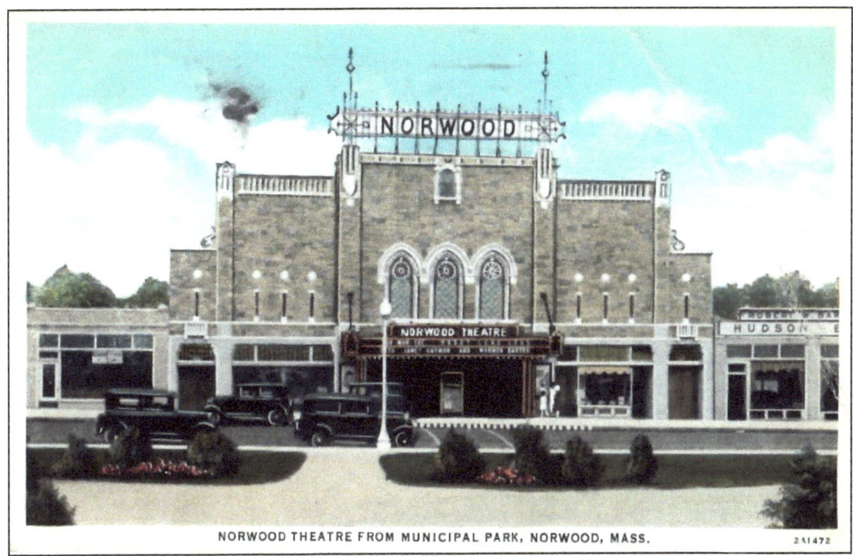

NORWOOD THEATRE FROM MUNICIPAL PARK, NORWOOD, MASS.

The Norwood Theatre was designed by William G. Upham in a Spanish Romanesque style using granite and limestone to complement the nearby municipal building, also designed by Upham. Its impressive interior featured marble terrazzo floors, a cathedral pipe organ, and elaborate ceiling and cornice decorations.

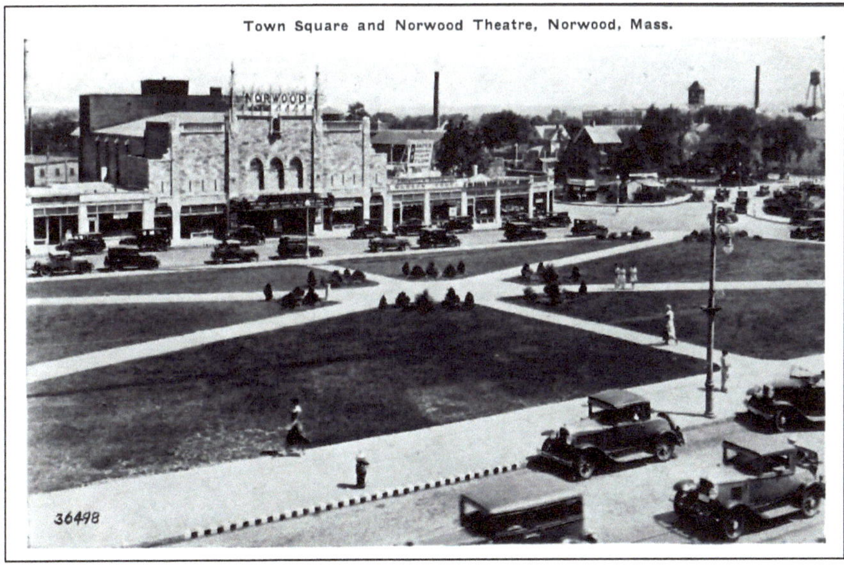

Town Square and Norwood Theatre, Norwood, Mass.

Opening to the public on August 31, 1927, and originally owned and operated by the Premiere Theatre Company, the Norwood Theatre has gone through many transformations. Still standing on the east side of the town square, the restored theatre today hosts theatrical, musical, and comedic performances.

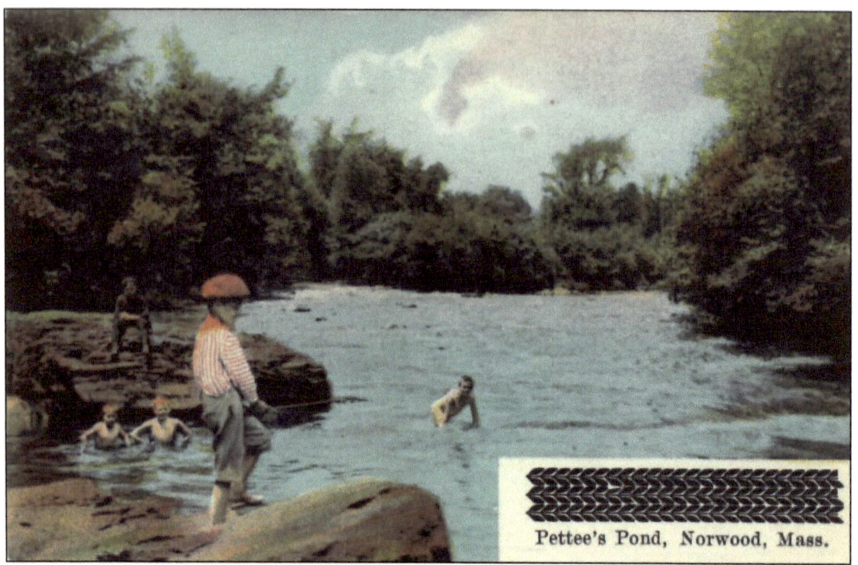

From its inception, South Dedham was nicknamed "Tiot," a word referring to native language meaning "enclosed by waters." Local waterways, including the Neponset River, and smaller streams, brooks, and ponds, have long been a source of recreation for the community. Pettee's Pond is one of these sites.

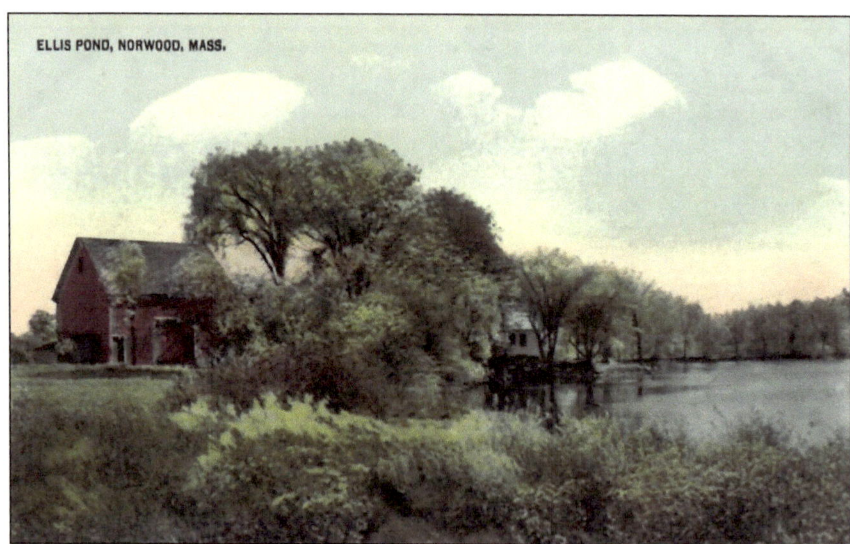

Ellis Pond was likely created to provide power for a paper mill in 1832. By mid-century, the Ellis family operated an ice harvesting business here. In February of 1972, the Town of Norwood purchased Ellis Pond. Modern improvements include clearing brush, constructing walking paths, and adding signage.

70

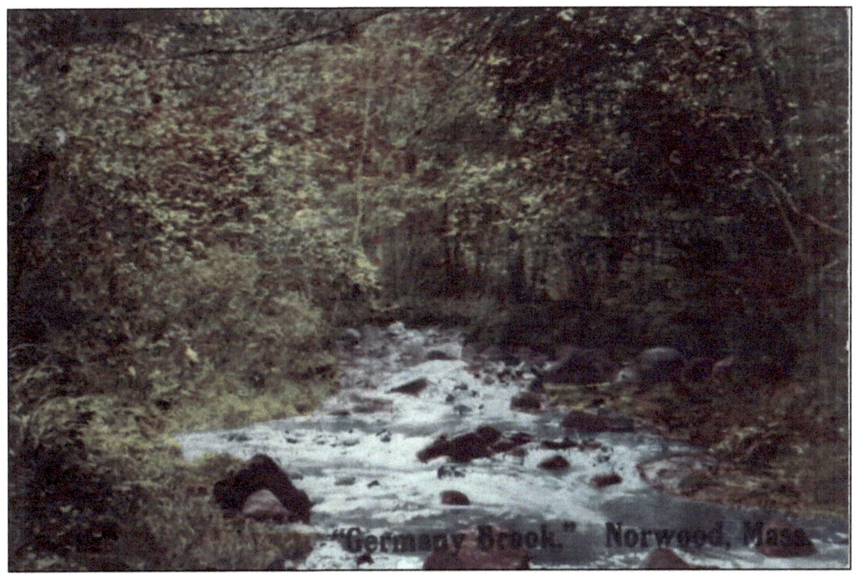

Germany Brook, so named because it ran through the southwest portion of South Dedham where German immigrants built their homes, was a popular local site for fishing and family picnics. Today subsumed by houses and roads, this postcard captures the wooded wilderness it once was.

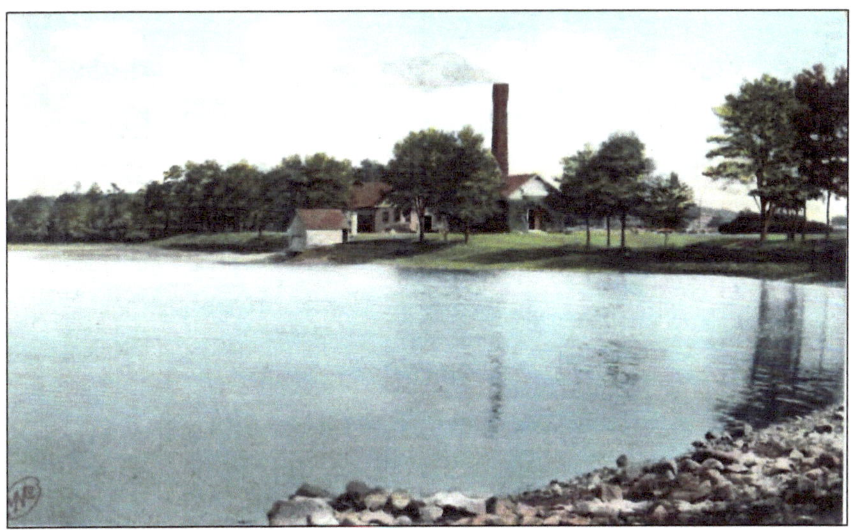

Another sometimes forgotten waterway, Buckmaster Pond is actually situated in Westwood. Norwood purchased the pond from the Commonwealth of Massachusetts in the late nineteenth century and erected a pumping station. Despite its use, the picturesque charm of the area made this image a popular one.

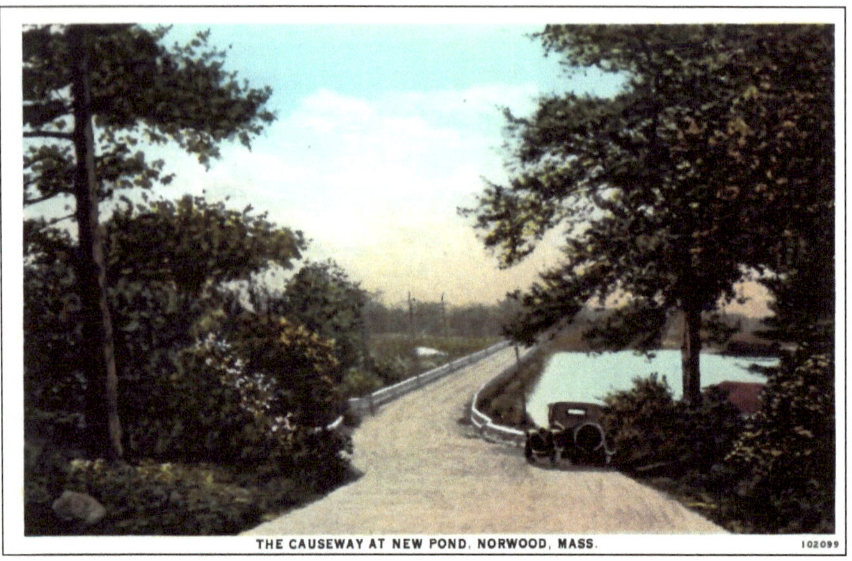

THE CAUSEWAY AT NEW POND, NORWOOD, MASS.

Willett Pond, known locally as New Pond, was created by George F. Willett as head of Winslow Brothers and Smith Company tannery. It immediately became one of Norwood's best scenic and recreational assets. This card depicts the newly built vehicular causeway at the water's edge.

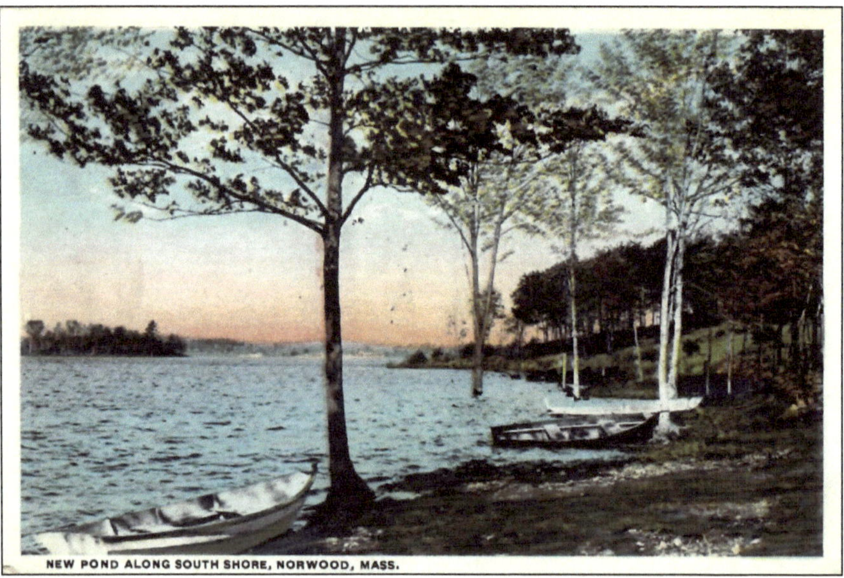

NEW POND ALONG SOUTH SHORE, NORWOOD, MASS.

Along the south shore of New Pond, no official piers or landings were needed for local residents to enjoy recreational boating. On the shores of nearby Pettee's Pond, a sawmill continued in operation until 1912 when Willett Pond was created.

72

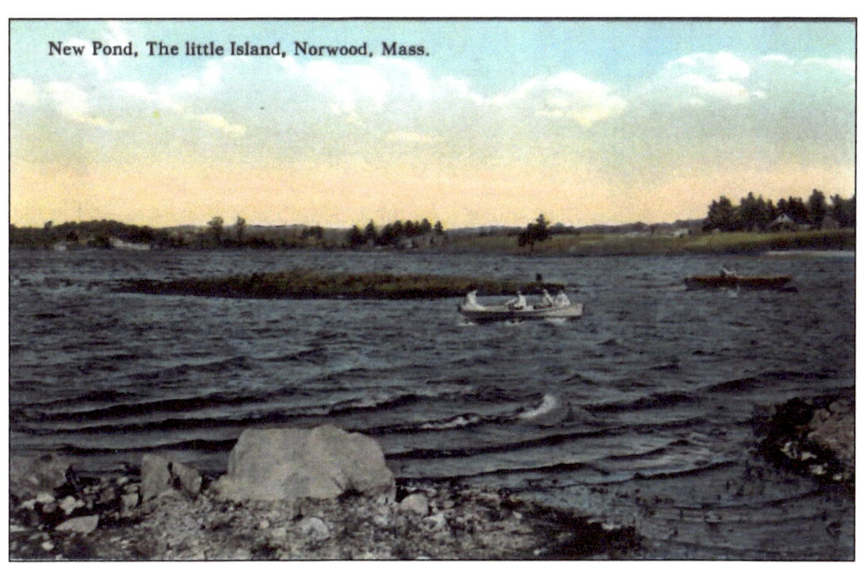

This image of Willett Pond includes not simply recreational row boats but the "little island" that emerged on occasion, depending on the water's depth. In wintertime, the pond was a popular ice skating and ice fishing location as well.

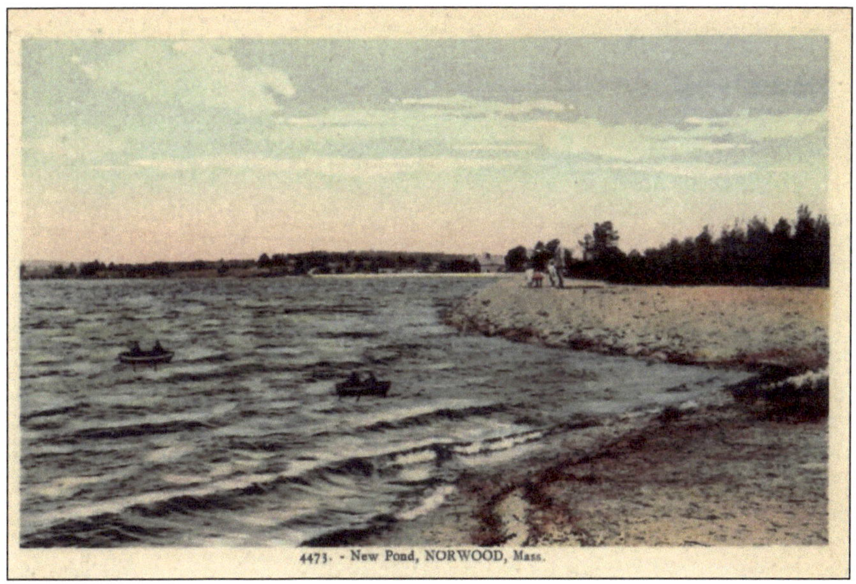

Small crafts make their way into the pond from the small beachhead that stood at the water's edge. Soon after Willett Pond was created, local residents began to gather in the summer for a refreshing swim at the rudimentary beach that encircled the water.

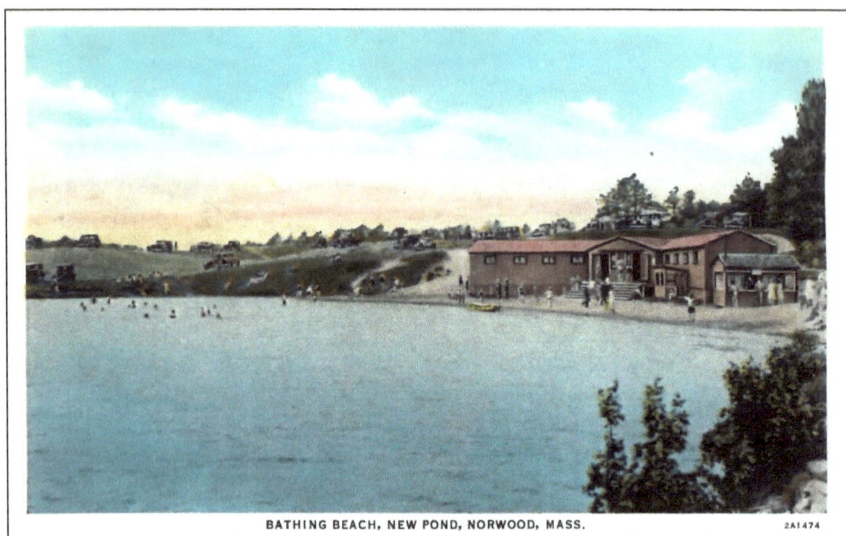

In June 1916, a public bathing area officially opened at Willett Pond. George F. Willett envisioned a housing development he called "Westover" stretching across his Norwood property; residents would have access to the pond. Eventually, Willett commissioned William G. Upham to design a bath house at the pond's beach.

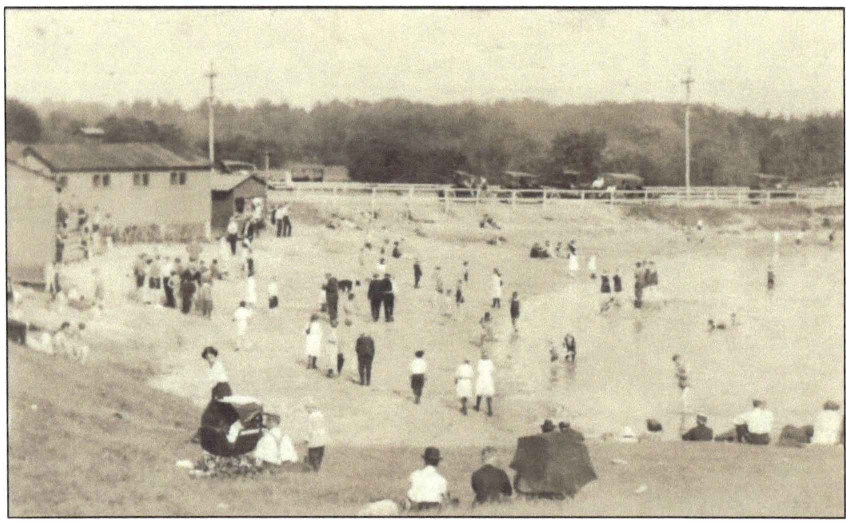

This view of Willett Pond by Norwood photographer C. L. Smith captures beach goers, the bath house, and, in the distance, the causeway. The Archdiocese of Boston purchased the property in the 1960s and established St. Timothy's Roman Catholic Church, ending public access to the beach and pond.

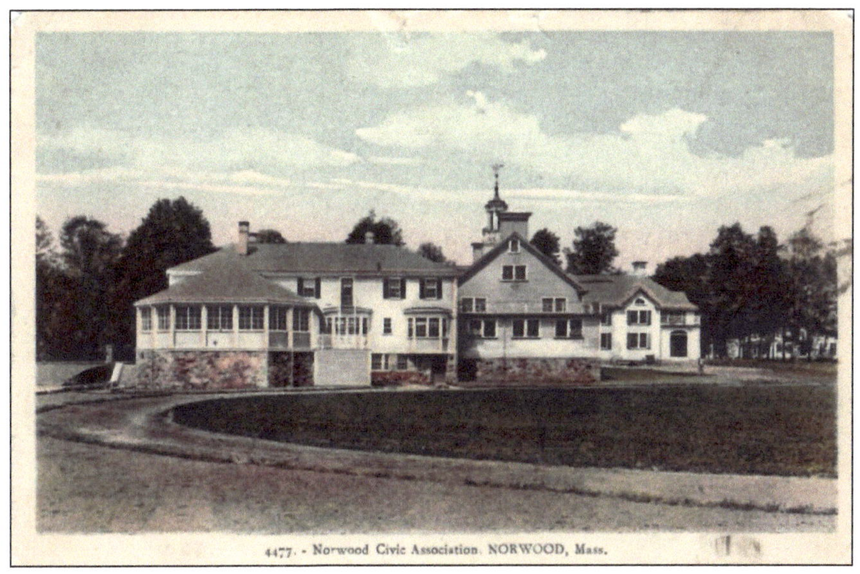

The Norwood Civic Association was the brainchild of entrepreneur George F. Willett. His clubhouse contained an auditorium, gymnasium, swimming pool, billiard room, bowling alley, social hall, and individual meeting rooms. There were exhibitions as well as instruction in English, citizenship, and homemaking.

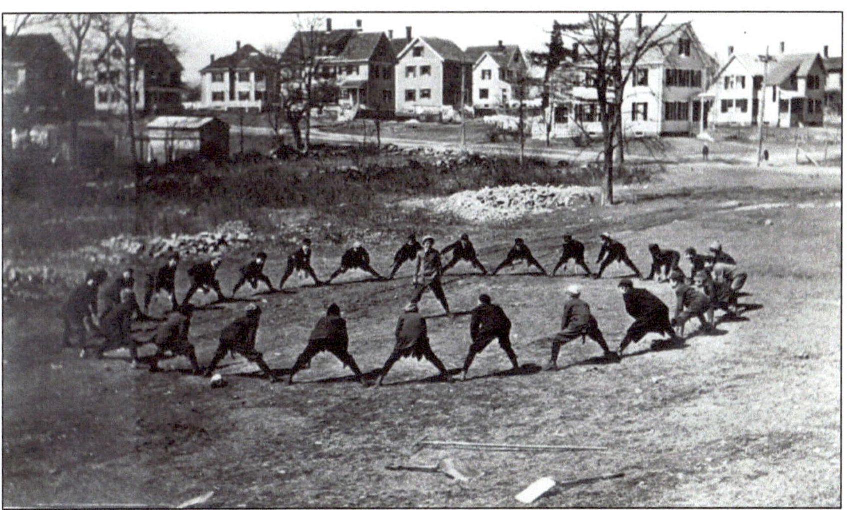

Outside, Willett constructed athletic fields and tennis courts. This view of an exercise class at the Civic was taken before the recreational complex was completed. After two fires severely damaged the building, Willett, who was facing financial problems of his own, sold the facility to the town in 1930.

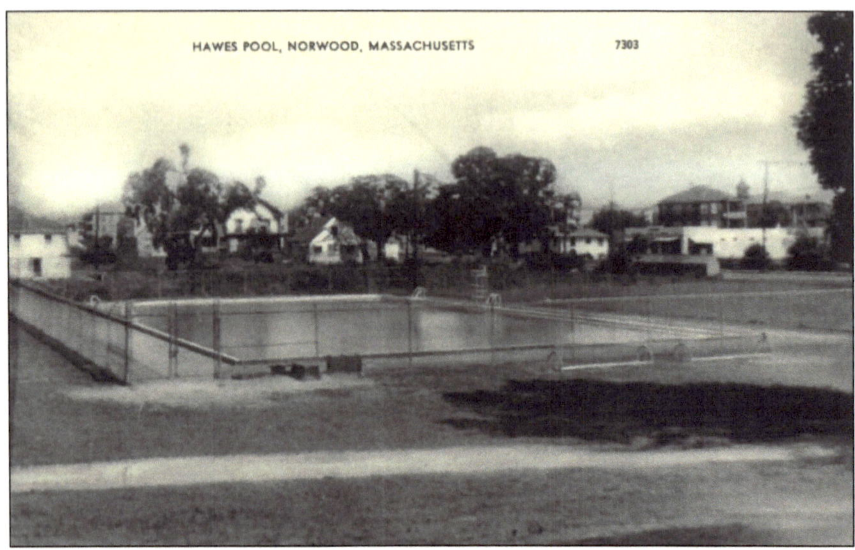

In South Norwood, on land formerly owned by Charles S. Bird, the acreage along Hawes Brook which eventually included a bath house and picnic site, was a popular summer site. Later Hawes Pool was constructed off Washington Street. The Hawes Pool complex remains there today.

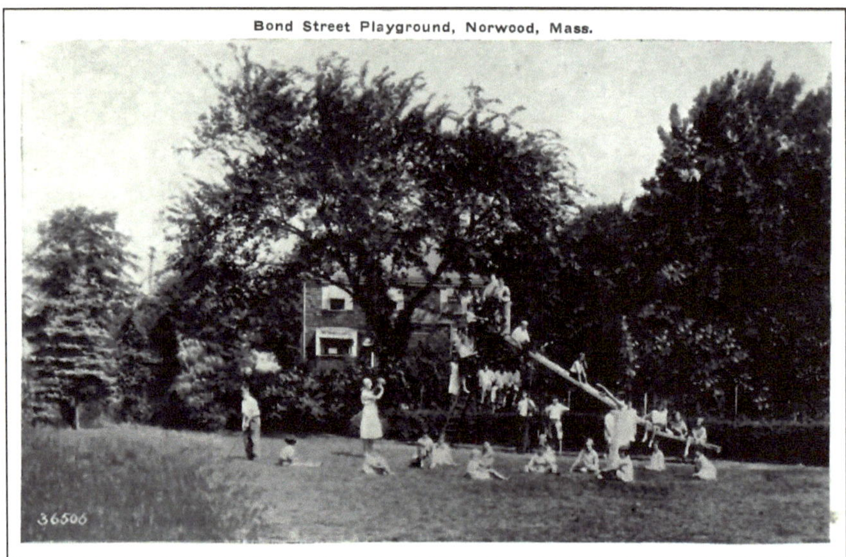

By the mid-twentieth century, the Norwood Recreation Department had replaced George F. Willett's Civic Association. Under their auspices, playgrounds were opened across Norwood. The Bond Street Playground, pictured here, was set on land that had been originally cleared by Frederick A. Cleveland, a long-time school committee member.

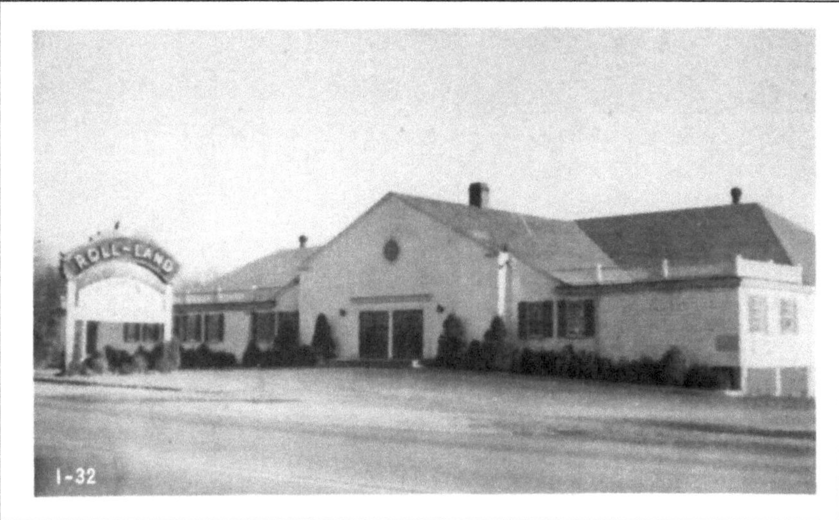

Founded by Charles, Peter, and John Santoro, Roll-Land opened on Thanksgiving Day in 1938. Located on Rte. 1 near Dean Street, Roll-Land Roller Rink and Bowling Alleys attracted couples, families, and serious athletes for decades. Following World War II, new-found respect for both speed and figure skating brought amateur productions and professional roller-skating competitions to Roll-Land. At the height of the rink's popularity, special buses transported skating enthusiasts to the skating emporium on Saturday nights. Skating festivals highlighted the efforts of student skaters of all ages and abilities, while dance competitions always drew a large audience. Among serious athletes of both speed and figure skating, Roll-Land and its members acquired an enviable reputation in local, state, and national contests. After a fire totally destroyed the building in 1962, Roll-Land was rebuilt. Forever a part of the town's history, the banquet to commemorate Norwood's Centennial was held here in 1972. The business closed in July 2000.

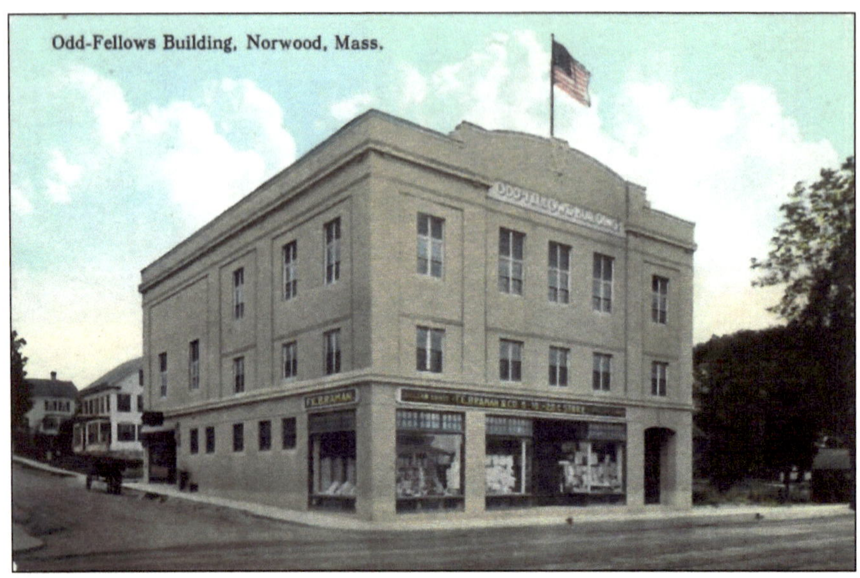

Founded in 1886, the fraternal Tiot Lodge of the Independent Order of Odd Fellows met in the Norwood House until Odd Fellows Hall was built and dedicated in 1913. It was architect William G. Upham's first commercial project. Today the exterior remains substantially unchanged.

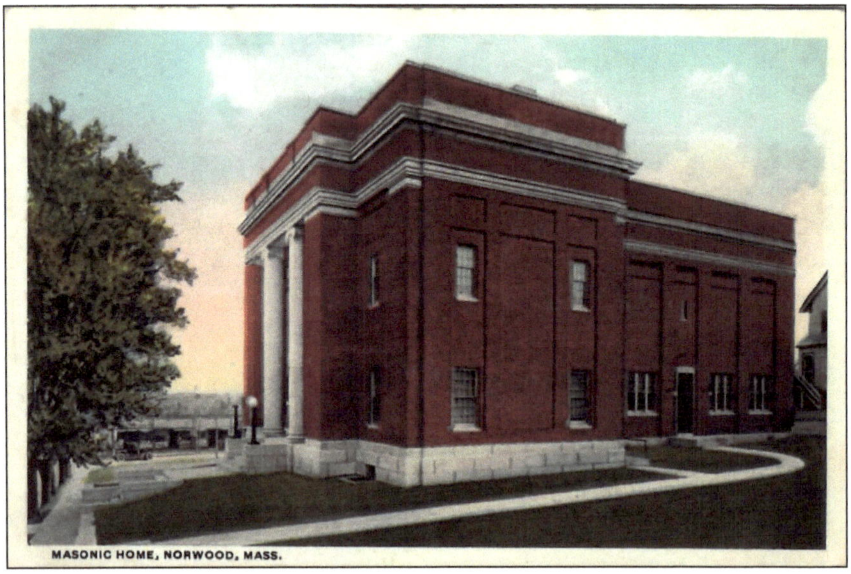

In 1916, the cornerstone of the Orient Lodge of Free and Accepted Masons was laid. Another Upham commission, the impressive two-story building of Harvard brick with Indiana limestone trim, is still the home of Norwood's Masons who continue to use it for meetings and other community activities.

Eight

BUSINESS & INDUSTRY

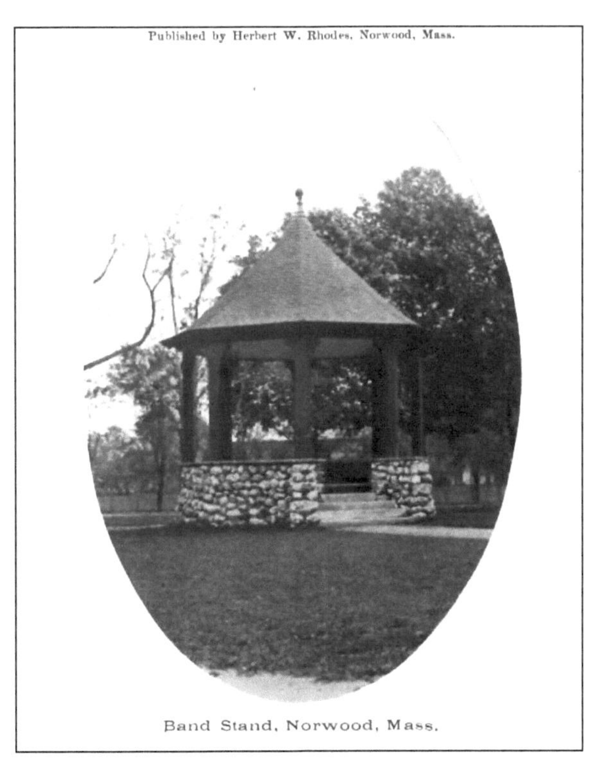

Band Stand, Norwood, Mass.

Norwood residents and brothers, Edward E. and Herbert W. Rhodes, opened a photography business on Cottage Street around 1905. They made a specialty of souvenir postcards, issuing postcard series for several area communities. The bandstand at Guild Square was one of the brothers' views of Norwood.

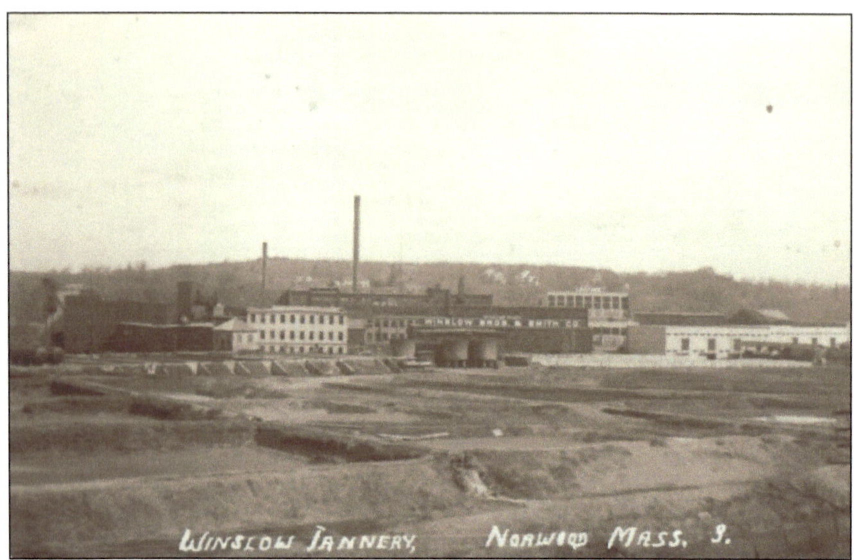

Founded by Abner Guild and later owned by John Smith, the tannery was divided into two successful operations by the sons of Lyman Smith and George Winslow. They stood at opposite ends of Norwood. This is a postcard of the Winslow tannery, off Endicott Street.

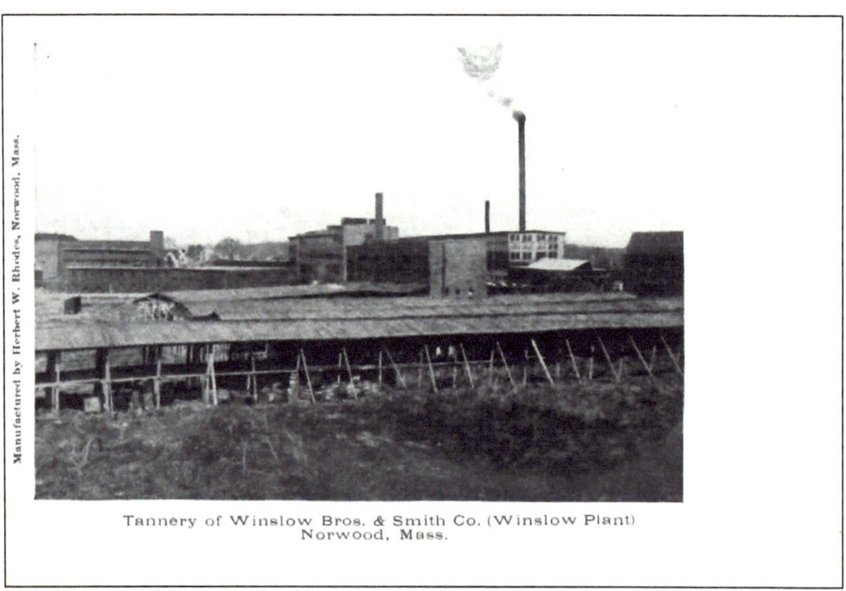

Tannery of Winslow Bros. & Smith Co. (Winslow Plant)
Norwood, Mass.

After the two tanneries were reunited under the direction of George F. Willett, the business became Winslow Bros. & Smith. One of Norwood's largest employers, the tannery finally closed c.1950. This image of the Winslow plant, off today's Endicott Street, was taken by the Rhodes brothers.

80

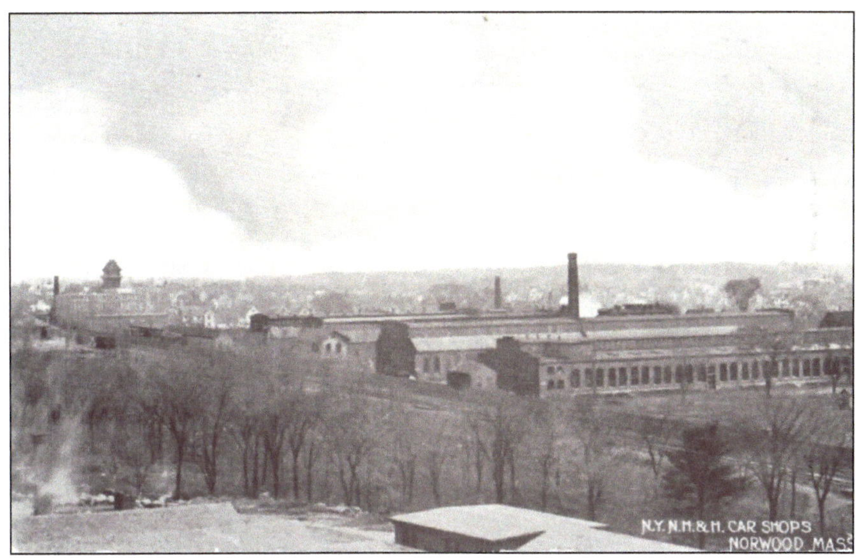

In 1876, the New York & New England Railroad relocated its building and repair shops from Readville to Norwood. In 1889, a steam locomotive maintenance facility was added to the plant which eventually employed over 300. The business returned to Readville in 1907.

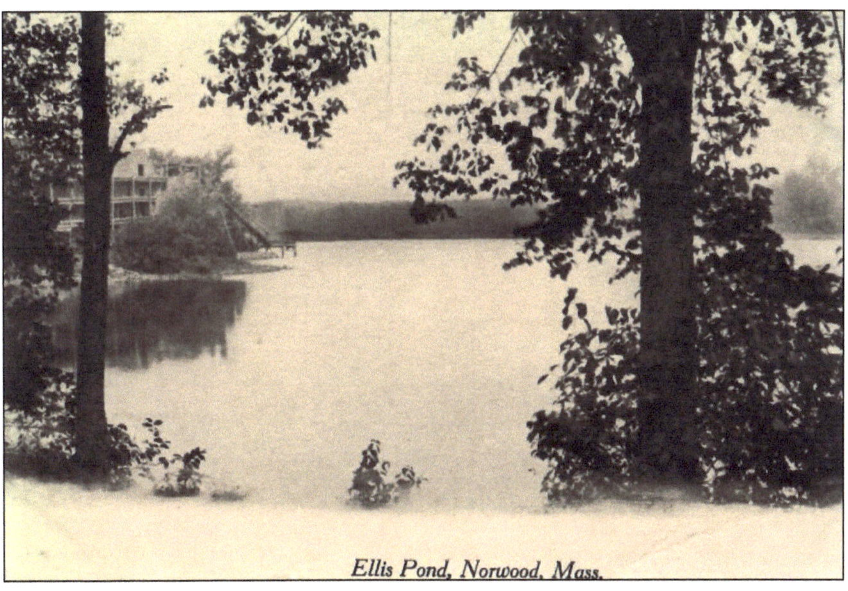

The harvesting of ice on Ellis Pond began in the 1860s. Eventually, the Norwood Ice Company and its icehouse, operated by the Ellis family, had a near monopoly in the business in Norwood and West Dedham. With the advent of refrigeration, the facility closed.

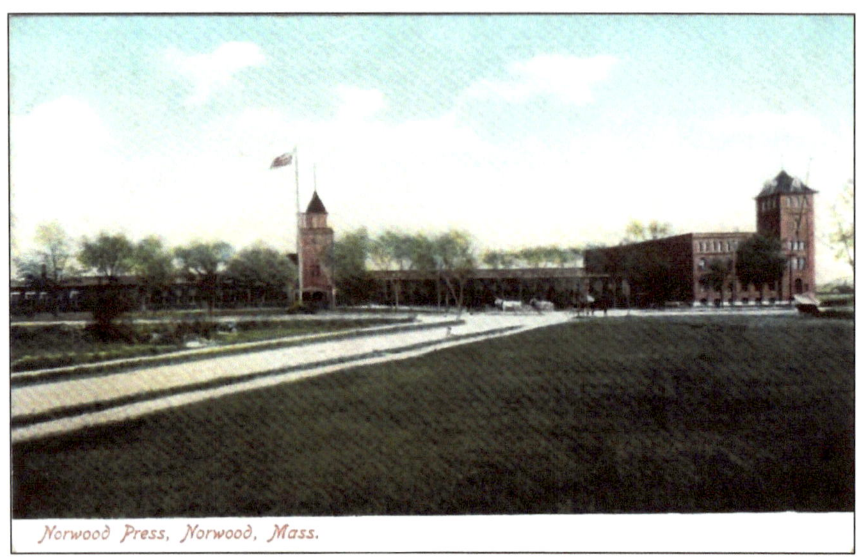

Charged with attracting businesses to town, the Norwood Business Association brought together three independent firms to form the Norwood Press. Although they remained separate entities, their collective business specialized in the complete fabrication of scientific, school and college textbooks, illustrated books, and pamphlets.

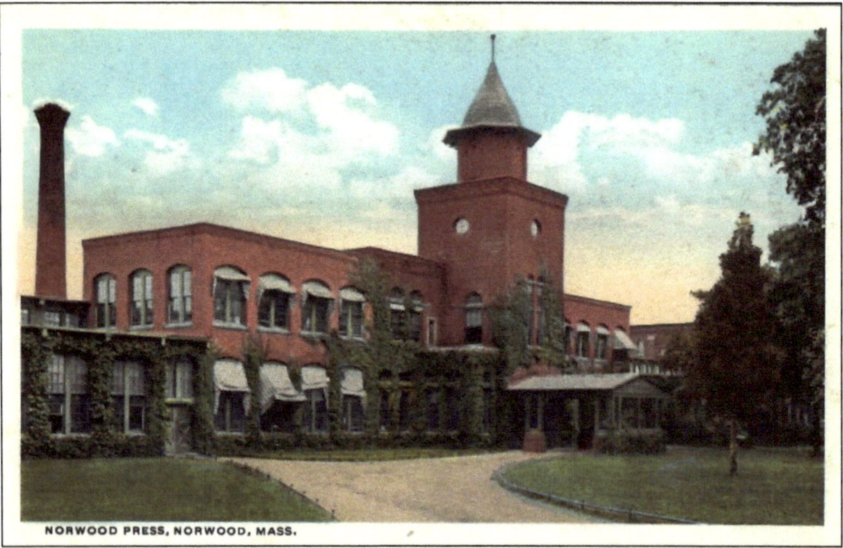

J. S. Cushing and Company was a composition and electrotyping foundry founded by its proprietor, J. Stearns Cushing, in 1878. The business arrived in Norwood in 1894 along with Berwick & Smith Company, a press room. The two were legally incorporated as the Norwood Press Company.

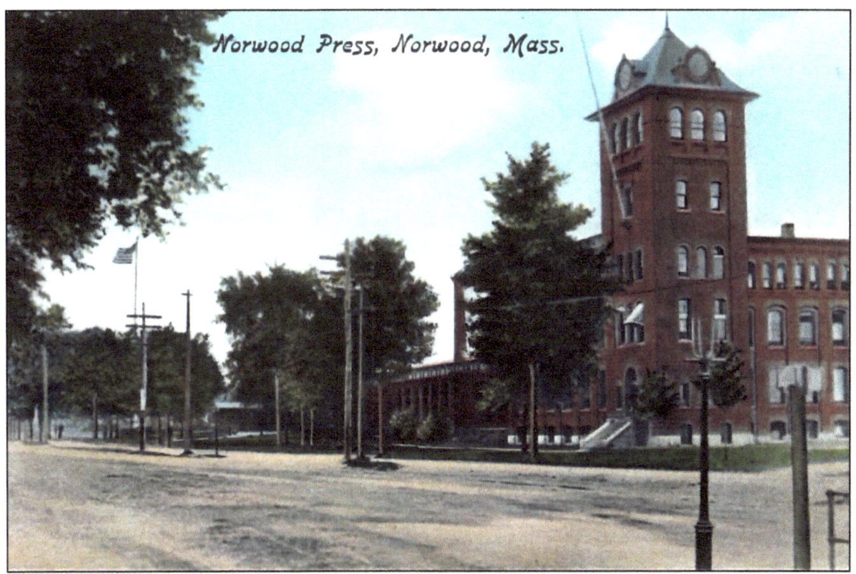

The two founding Norwood Press concerns were joined by the E. Fleming Company, one of the oldest binderies in New England, in 1897. The Press conglomerate, located in a striking and expansive facility on Washington Street at Walnut Avenue, eventually employed over 700 workers.

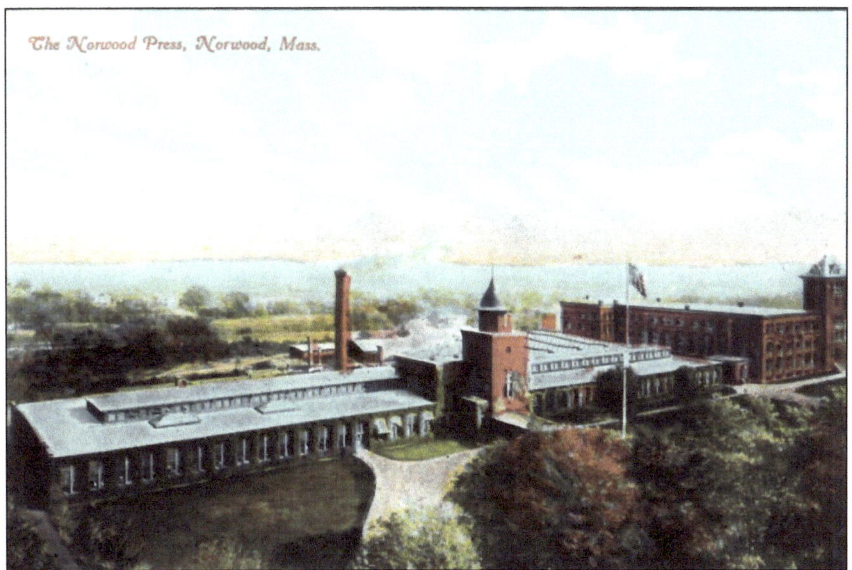

In addition to joint book fabrication, each business maintained its own customer base. The conglomerate's chief customers remained the publishing houses in New York and Boston. After World War II, a decline in production and labor disputes caused the Norwood Press to dissolve in the early 1950s.

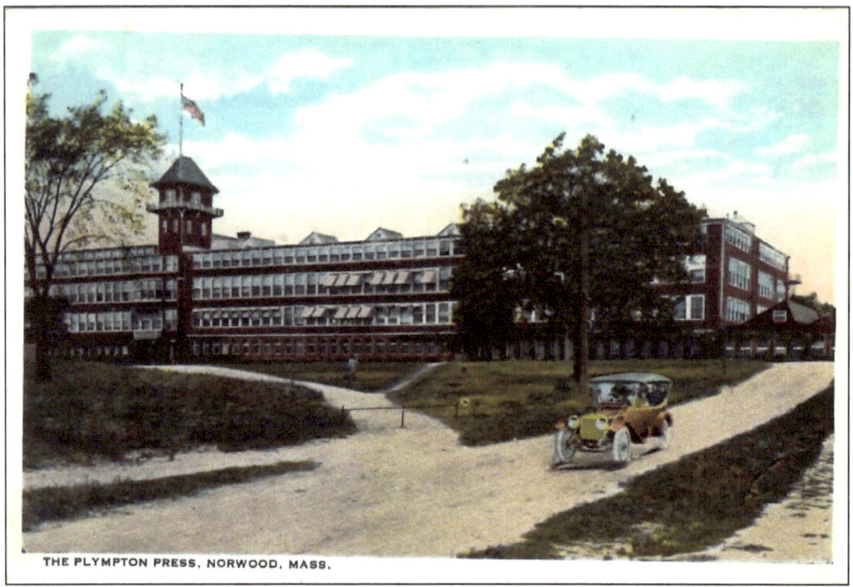

Enhancing Norwood's reputation as a bookmaking center was the Plimpton Press, founded by Herbert M. Plimpton and his brother Howard. In 1897, the Boston-based Plimpton Press moved its press work and binding operations to a site east of the town center at Lenox and Nahatan Streets.

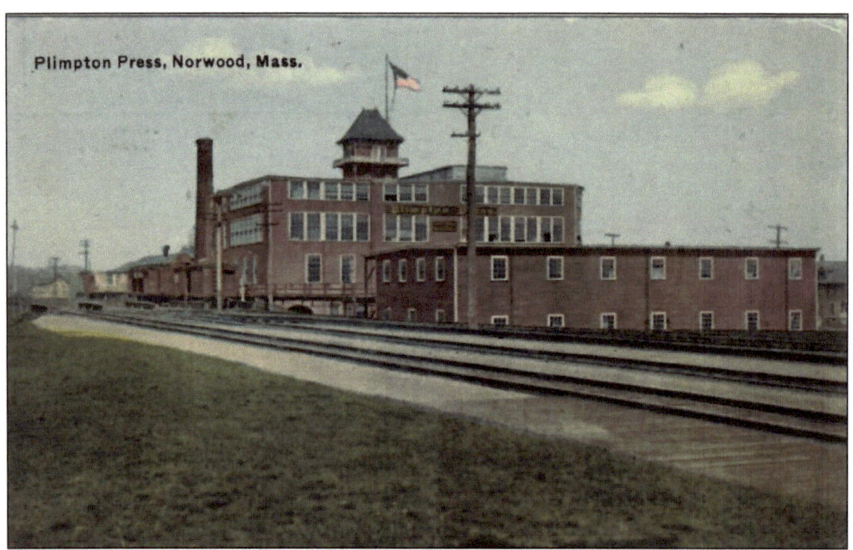

In 1904, Herbert Plimpton brought the remainder of his Boston business to Norwood and, by 1905, the firm, known as H. M. Plimpton and Company, employed close to 600. In conjunction with the Norwood Press, this move made Norwood a center of book production in America.

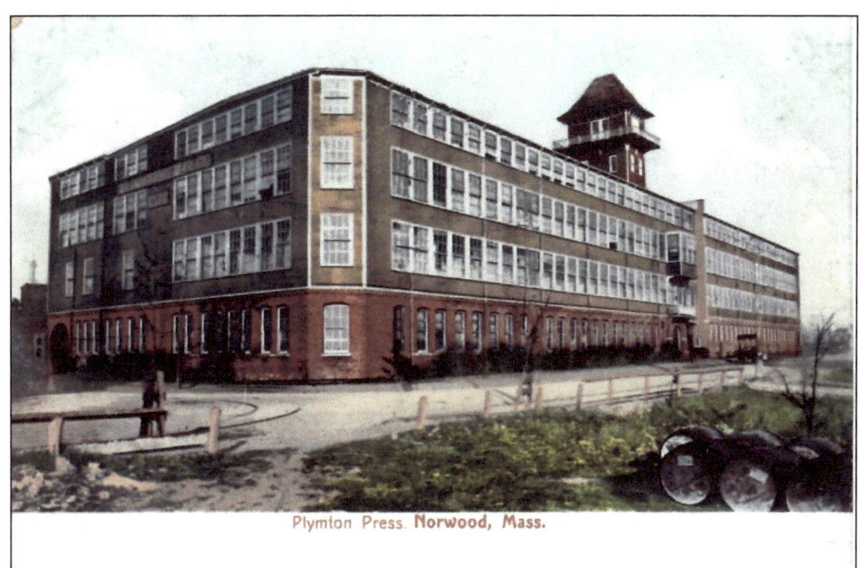

While the typesetting, presswork, and binding elements of book production were completed in the Plimpton plant, the fabrication of book cloth and binding material was the work of Holliston Mills, an adjunct business of the Plimpton family. Although book cloth continued to be its most important product, Holliston Mills eventually manufactured window-shade material, broadcloth, and map cloths as well. It was finally incorporated as a separate entity in the 1920s when the press was itself incorporated as the Plimpton Press. Together the businesses employed more than 1,000 local workers. Initially, most of Plimpton's business derived from textbook publishing but fiction, reference works, and religious books were later added to the production schedule. At its peak, Plimpton's could roll 50,000 volumes off its presses daily. Eventually production shifted to other locations in the U.S., and by 1960, Plimpton's had ceased manufacturing in Norwood. Eventually, the business offices departed as well. Today, the site is an Avalon apartment complex.

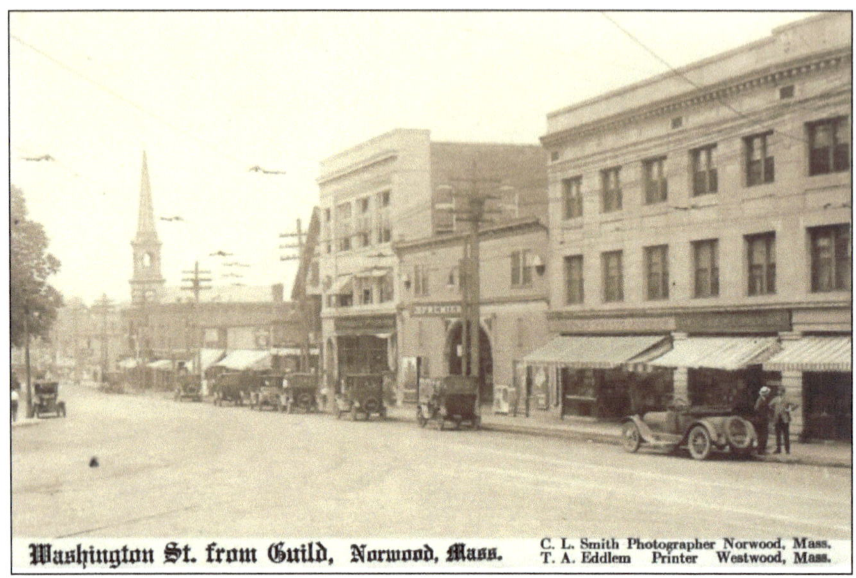

Local men Charles L. Smith and T. A. Eddlem joined forces to produce a series of postcards in the early twentieth century. This view, looking north on Norwood center, shows the Talbot Block, the Premiere Theatre, the Callahan Building, and, in the distance, the First Baptist Church.

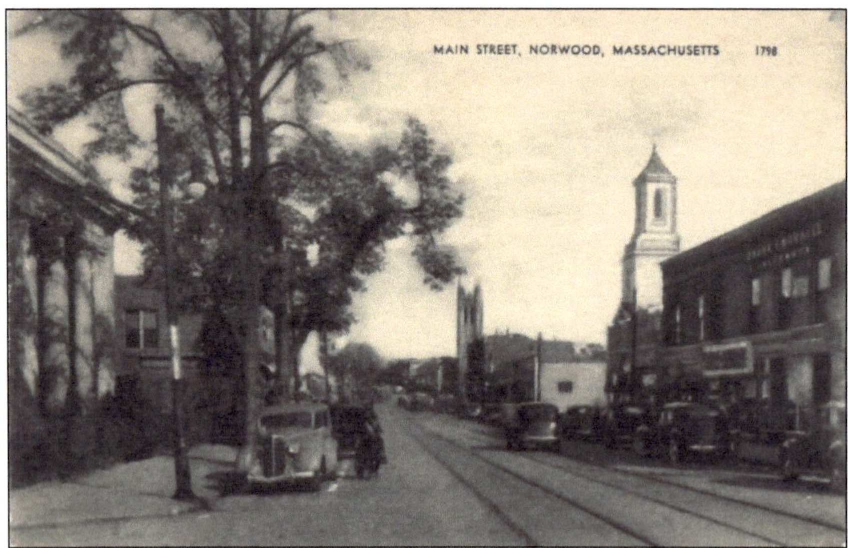

After the hurricane of 1938 toppled its steeple, the First Baptist Church was repaired with a new steeple. This view of Washington Street, looking north from Day Street, shows the transformation and the encroachment of commercial buildings. The town hall can be seen in the distance.

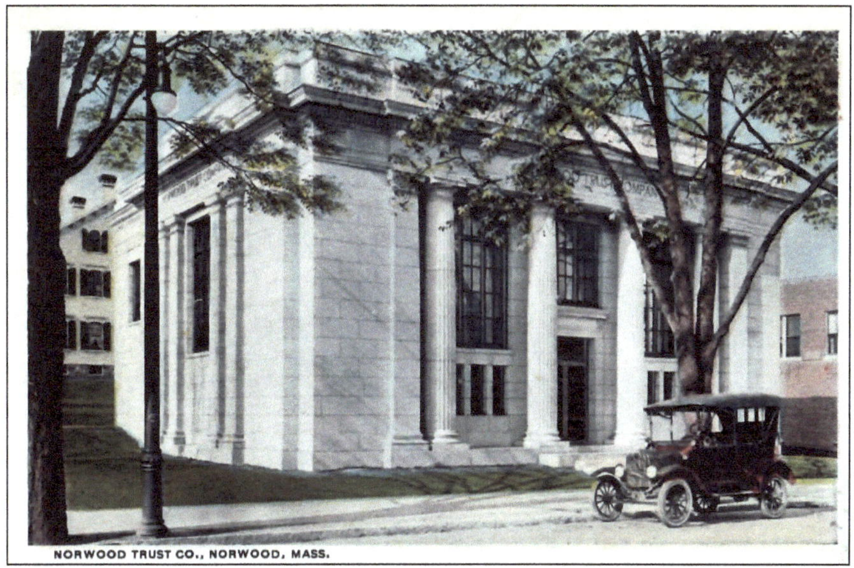

In 1917, the Norwood Trust Company with George F. Willett as president, moved into this handsome Neo-Classical style building. It was subsequently home to several banking establishments. Although no longer a financial institution, the building still stands at the corner of Washington and Day Streets.

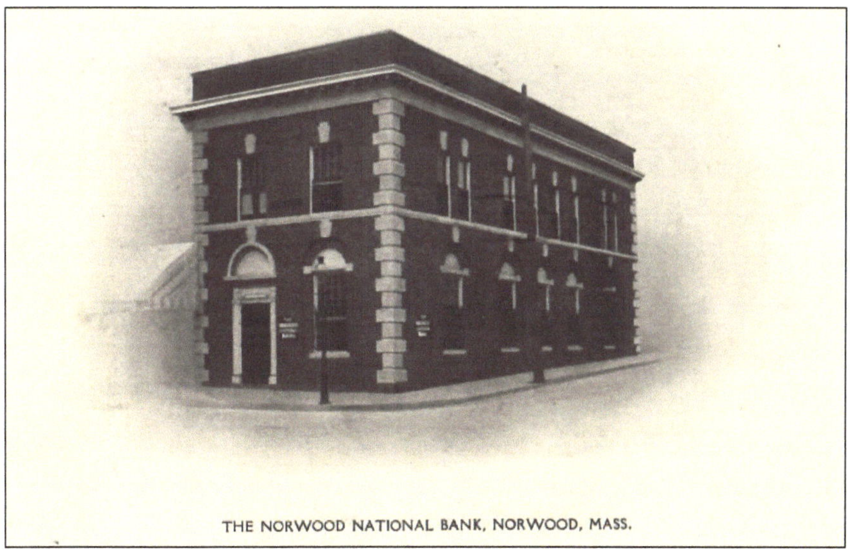

Initially the home of the Norwood National Bank (which became the Norwood Trust Company), and later the Norwood Morris Plan Company, which pioneered the concept of consumer credit to working class families, this portion of the Sanborn Block has served as retail space for decades.

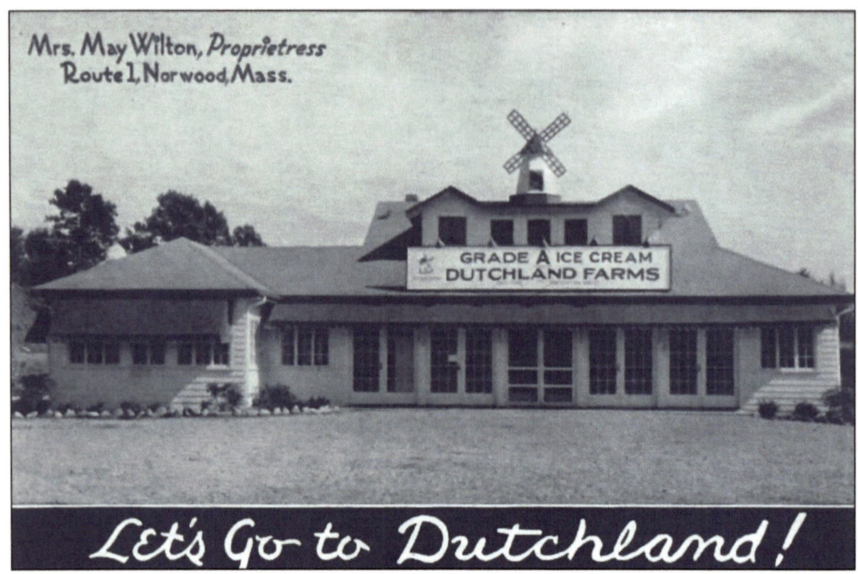

Dutchland Farms was a regional distributor of dairy products based in Brockton, with locations throughout eastern Massachusetts. Each produced similar postcards with the proprietor's name and address in the corner. Norwood's Dutchland stood at the corner of Cross Street and U.S. Route 1.

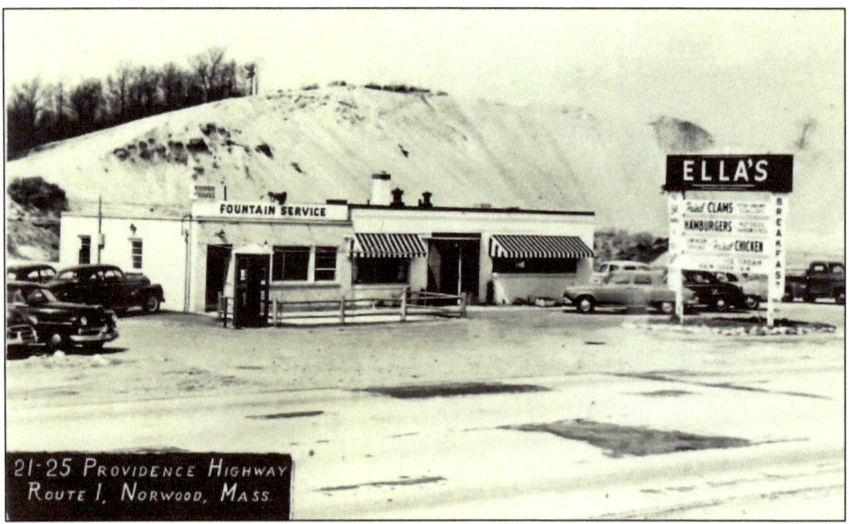

By 1937 the Boston-Providence Highway (U. S. Route 1) went through to New York, making the roadway ever more popular. Ella's, located at the highway's intersection with Everett Street, offered fried clams, fried chicken, hamburgers, and fountain service to its customers. Ed O'Toole's sandpit is visible behind the building.

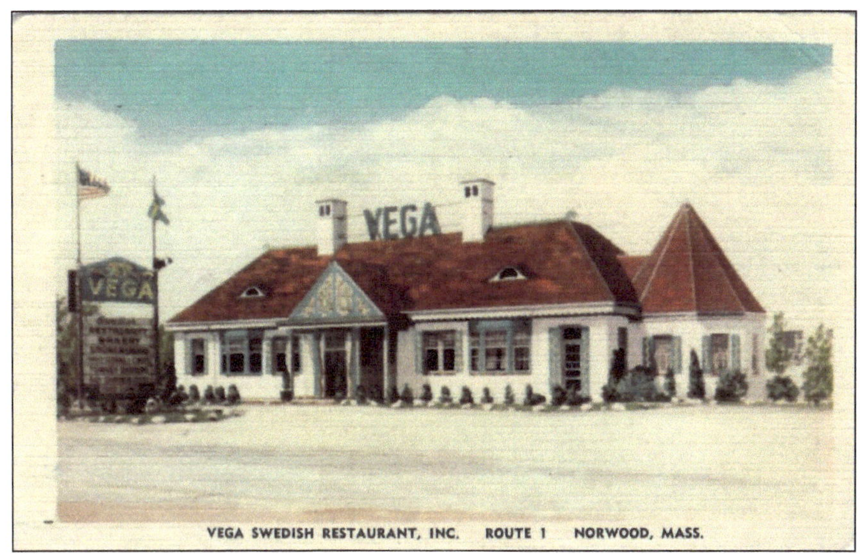

Vega Swedish Restaurants advertised themselves as "nationally famous for outstanding Swedish-American menus." Located on U.S. Route 1 near Dean Street, Norwood's Vega restaurant offered "authentic" Swedish coffee served in copper pots. The site was later home to the Honolulu restaurant; today, a Walgreen's stands there.

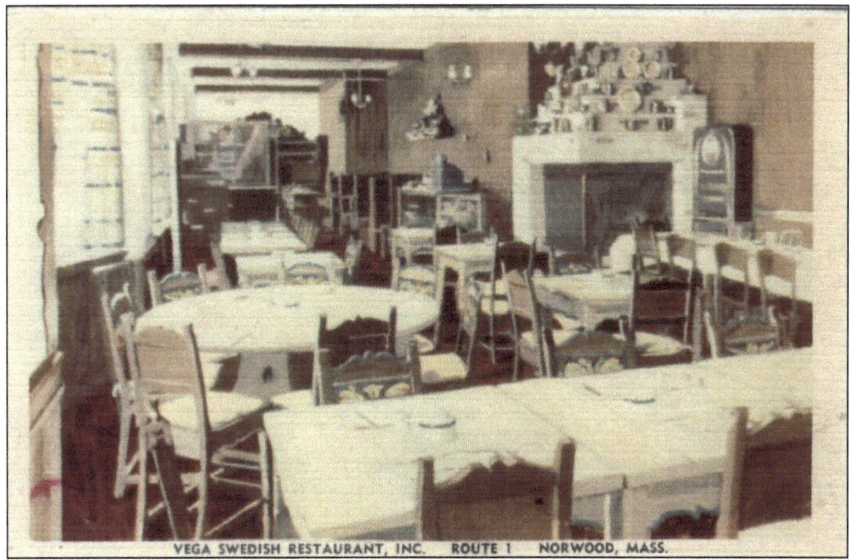

The interior of the Vega restaurant was decorated in a comfortable manner attractive to family gatherings and casual diners. The menu was varied. In 1949, a seafood dinner including soup, potato, vegetables, bread and butter, dessert, and coffee was $1.35.

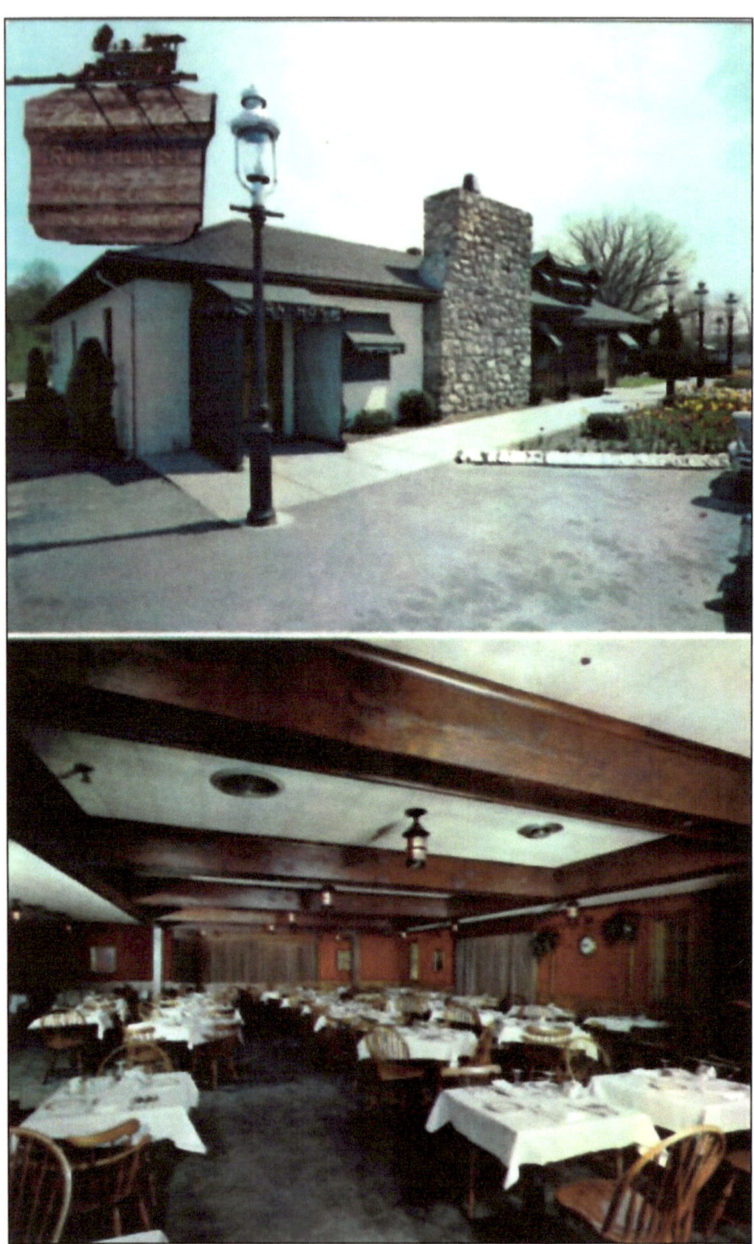

Founded by John Cornetta and known as Cornetta's Iron Horse, this restaurant stood for decades on U.S. Route 1 in Norwood not far from the rotary between Nahatan and Neponset Streets. Calling itself "New England's most exquisite restaurant, in an atmosphere of elegance," the Iron Horse sported a dark, paneled interior. It was the local spot for special events. The building has been demolished.

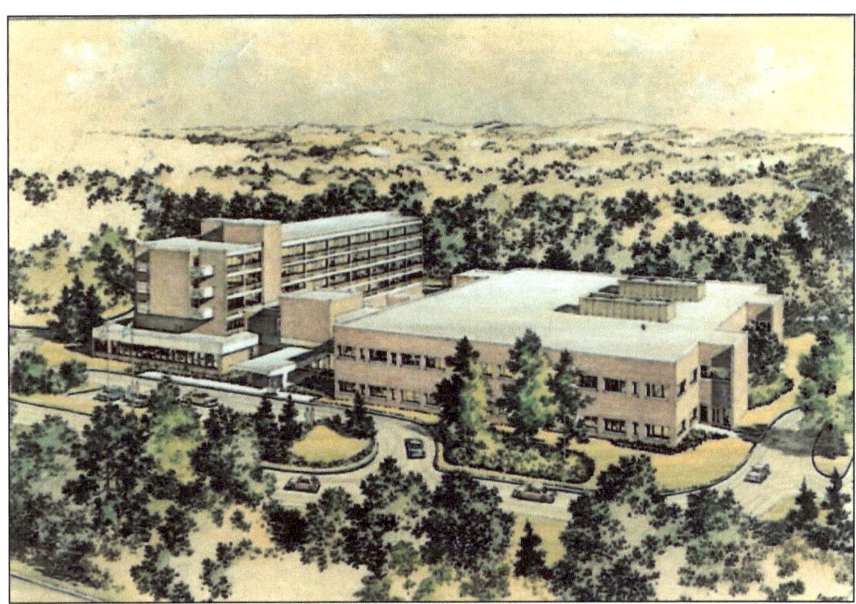

Opened in 1980, Factory Mutual's Conference Center on U.S. Route 1 in Norwood was billed as "one of the country's most advanced locations for seminars and meetings." The complex had 126 overnight accommodations, 24 meeting rooms, a dining room, lounge, and recreation facilities.

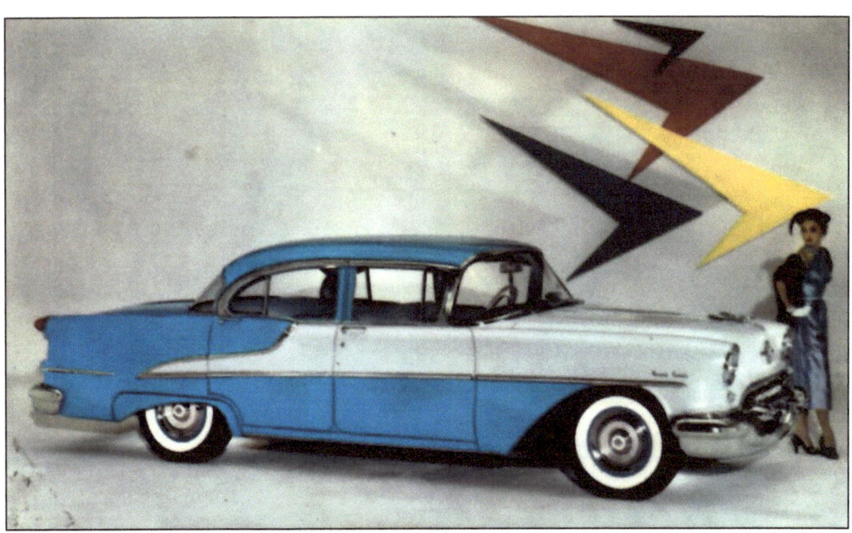

With the opening of U. S. Route 1, several auto dealerships gathered on the stretch of highway in Norwood that is still known as the "Automile." Even earlier, this postcard, distributed by Johnson Motor Sales of 354 Washington Street in Norwood, was a harbinger of things to come.

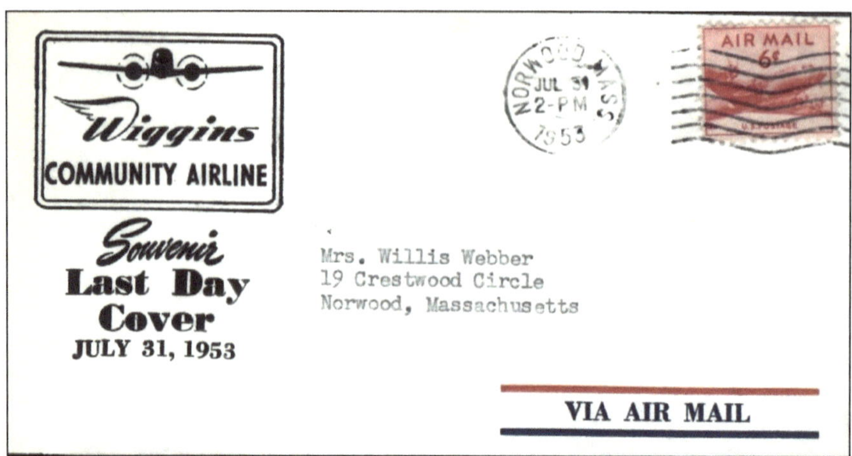

Although not a postcard, this souvenir Last Day Cover mailed on July 31, 1953, to commemorate Wiggins Community Airline is another piece of postal history. No longer operated by Wiggins Airways, the Norwood Memorial Airport remains a vibrant enterprise offering general aviation services. From the age of horse-drawn wagons, to railroads, trolleys, automobiles and air travel, the town of Norwood has maintained its hold on all manner of transportation.

NOVELTIES & GREETINGS

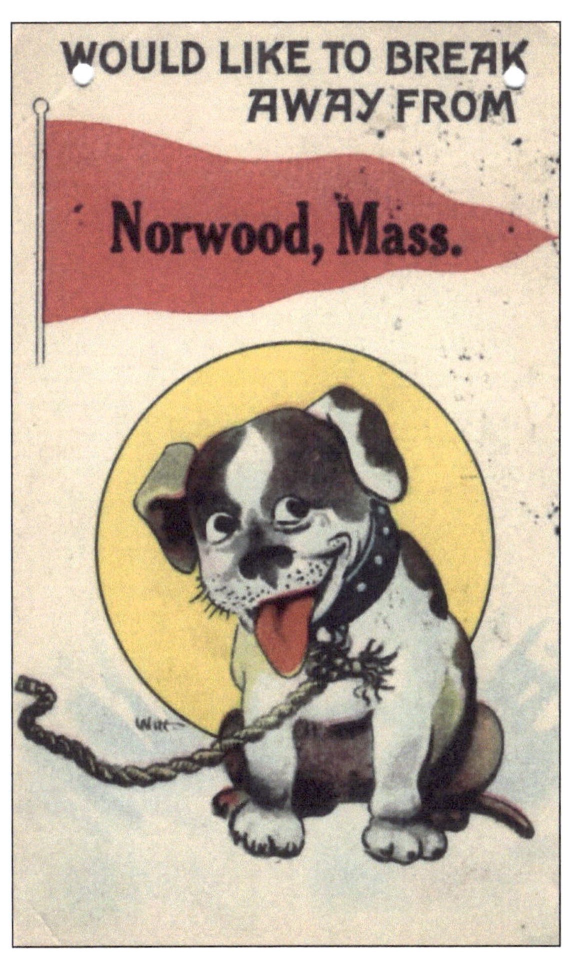

Most postcards were used to promote a town. Scenic views abounded, as did photos of businesses and homes. But some postcards were created simply as novelties. They were cartoon-like depictions expressing a variety of sentiments. Aiming at humor, the names of the locations or communities were interchangeable.

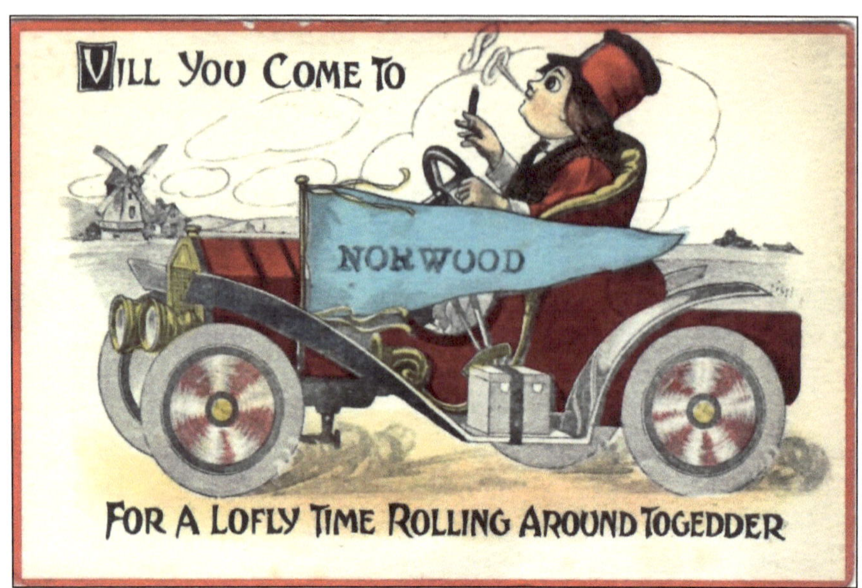

The message on the reverse echoes the sentiment on this postcard's face: "If you come Saturday, try and arrive here on the car that gets in at 5.40." The writer, named Lillian, is sending the card to her friend Ethel in faraway Canton Junction.

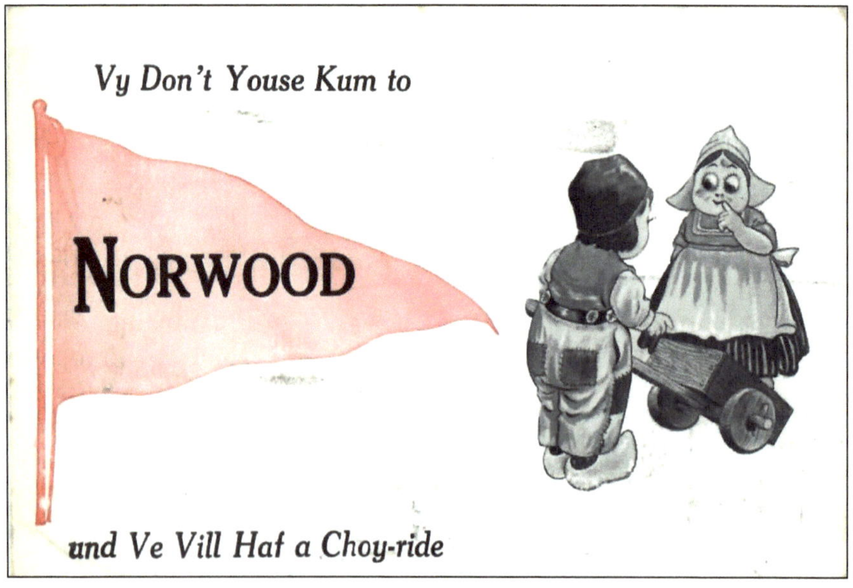

Postcards with messages written in exaggerated dialect were common in the early twentieth century. Again, the name of any town could be inserted in the banner. This card was sent in 1912.

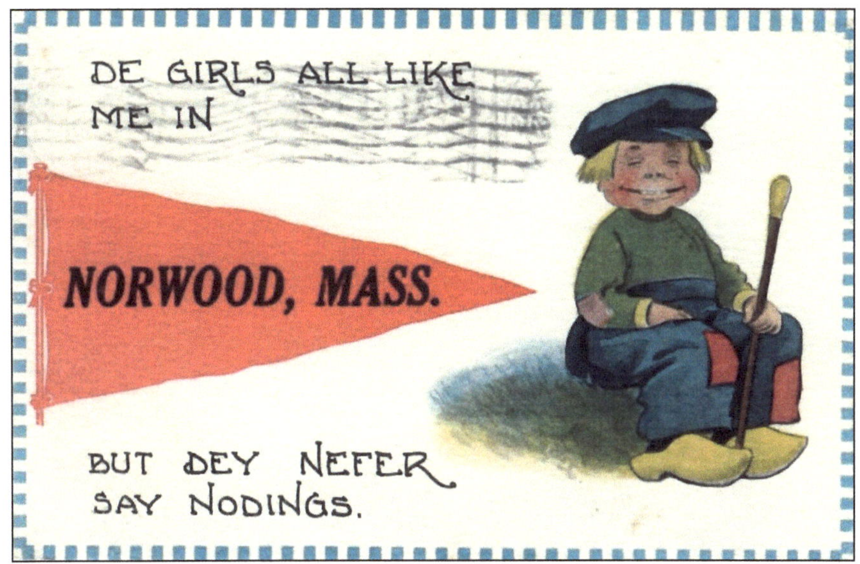

Banners and pennants, often in bright orange, were common on postcards issued in the 1910s and 1920s. They were used as a quick and inexpensive way to send a message. This card was sent to Alice Pratt in Manchester, New Hampshire, by her grandmother in Norwood.

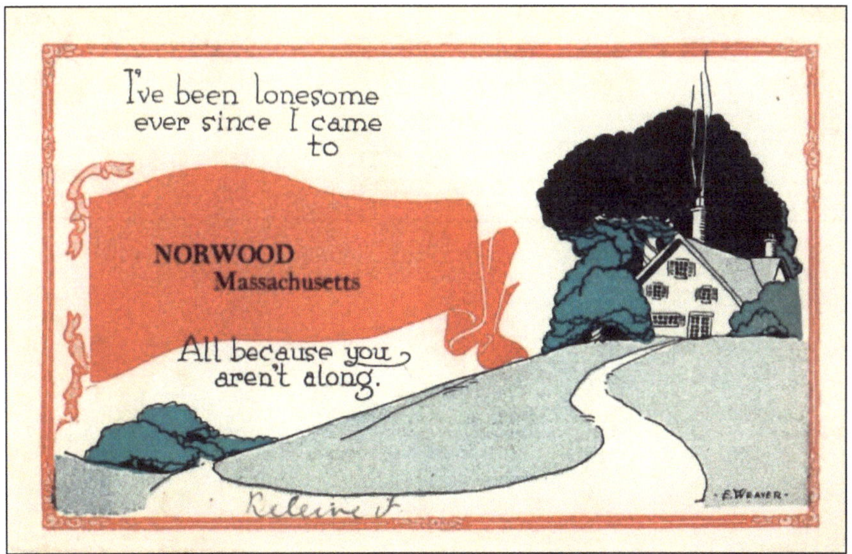

E. Weaver, the artist of this landscape message pennant card, signed the image. And if the message, "I've been lonesome ever since I came to Norwood, Massachusetts. All because you aren't along." was not clear enough, the sender has added "Believe it" in her own hand.

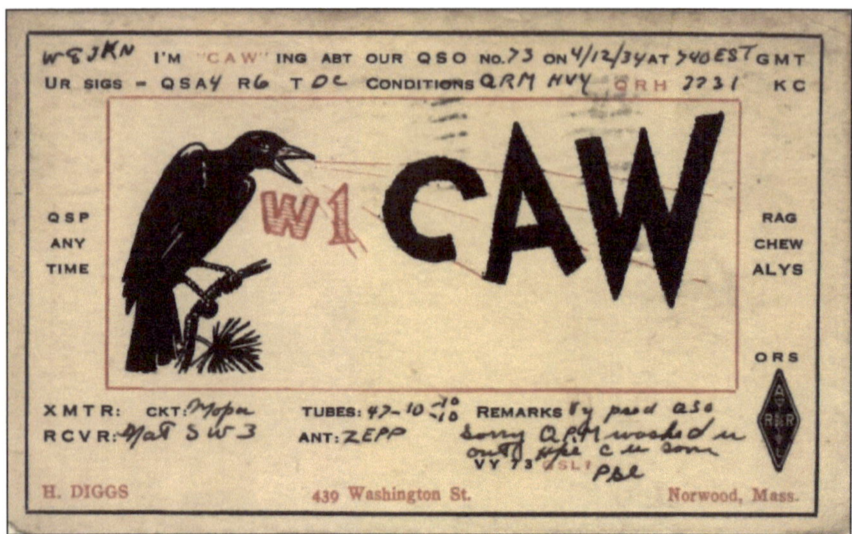

The term "ham" was initially a pejorative term used in the nineteenth century to mock telegraph operators with poor Morse code-sending skills. The term continued to be used after the invention of radio when wireless hobbyists were considered a nuisance by professionals. The amateur radio community subsequently reclaimed the word as a label of pride. Ham radio enthusiasts often sent postcards with their call signs to fellow operators. This card, sent by Henry Diggs of Norwood in 1934, contained an imaginative drawing along with technical details.

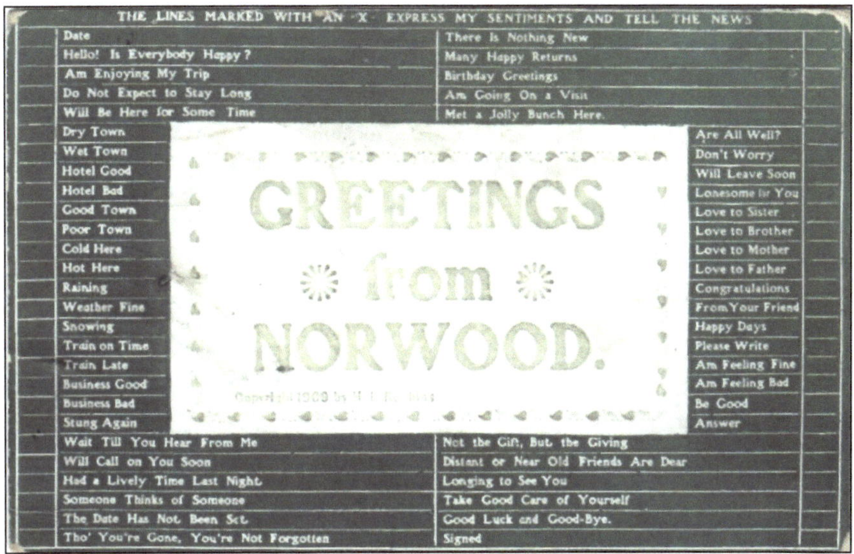

Date	There Is Nothing New
Hello! Is Everybody Happy?	Many Happy Returns
Am Enjoying My Trip	Birthday Greetings
Do Not Expect to Stay Long	Am Going On a Visit
Will Be Here for Some Time	Met a Jolly Bunch Here.

Dry Town		Are All Well?
Wet Town		Don't Worry
Hotel Good		Will Leave Soon
Hotel Bad		Lonesome for You
Good Town		Love to Sister
Poor Town		Love to Brother
Cold Here		Love to Mother
Hot Here		Love to Father
Raining		Congratulations
Weather Fine		From Your Friend
Snowing		Happy Days
Train on Time		Please Write
Train Late		Am Feeling Fine
Business Good		Am Feeling Bad
Business Bad		Be Good
Stung Again		Answer

Wait Till You Hear From Me	Not the Gift, But the Giving
Will Call on You Soon	Distant or Near Old Friends Are Dear
Had a Lively Time Last Night	Longing to See You
Someone Thinks of Someone	Take Good Care of Yourself
The Date Has Not Been Set	Good Luck and Good-Bye.
Tho' You're Gone, You're Not Forgotten	Signed

This type of "Greetings" card had a 1909 copyright. It cleverly included directions to place an "X" next to the intended sentiments such as "Will Call on You Soon," Weather Fine," "Love to Mother," and "Take Good Care of Yourself." Detailed news could be written on the reverse.

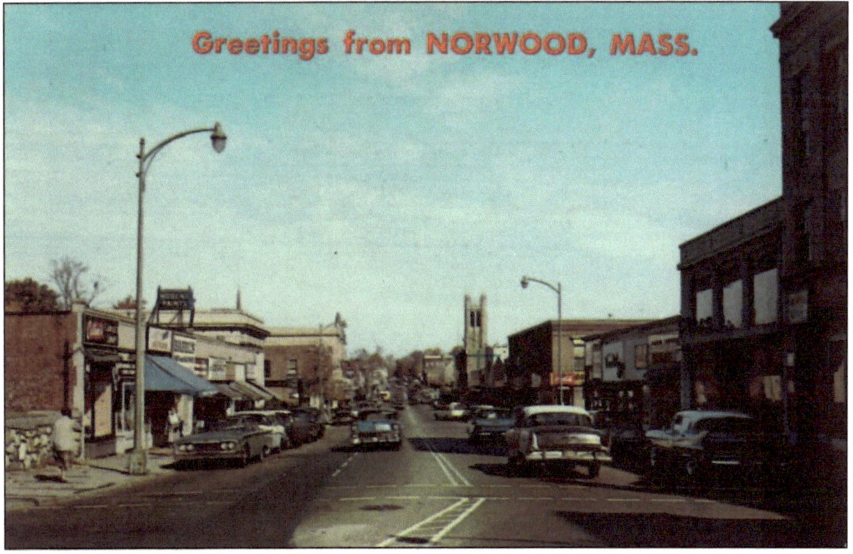

This is a twentieth century snapshot of Norwood's business district. Still recognizable are the Callahan Building (now a parking lot), the Bigelow Block, Norwood Trust Company, the Sanborn Block, and the Odd Fellows Building. Although the First Baptist Church is gone, the Memorial Municipal Building retains its landmark status.

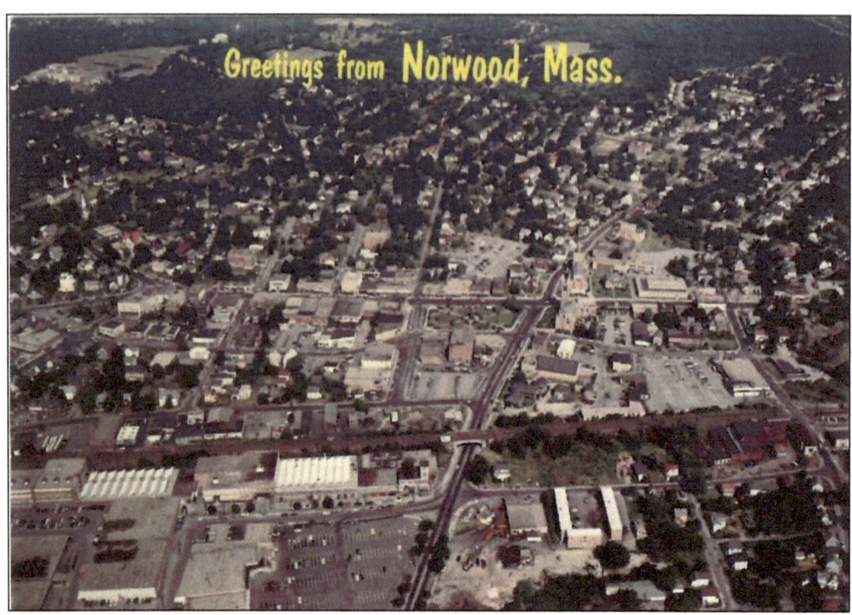

Taken in 1972 during Norwood's Centennial celebration, these two aerial views of Norwood were commissioned by the Norwood Co-Operative Bank. Some fifty years later, many structures – the Morrill Memorial Library, the Talbot Block at Guild Square, and the Town Hall – can still be identified. Others, like the Norwood Hospital complex, are no longer. The bank itself, reorganized as One Local, remains a community institution.

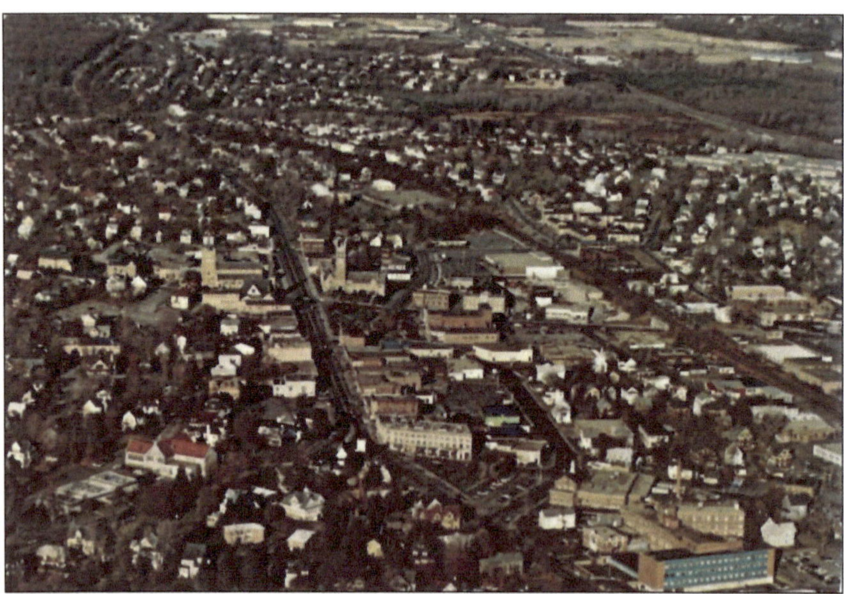

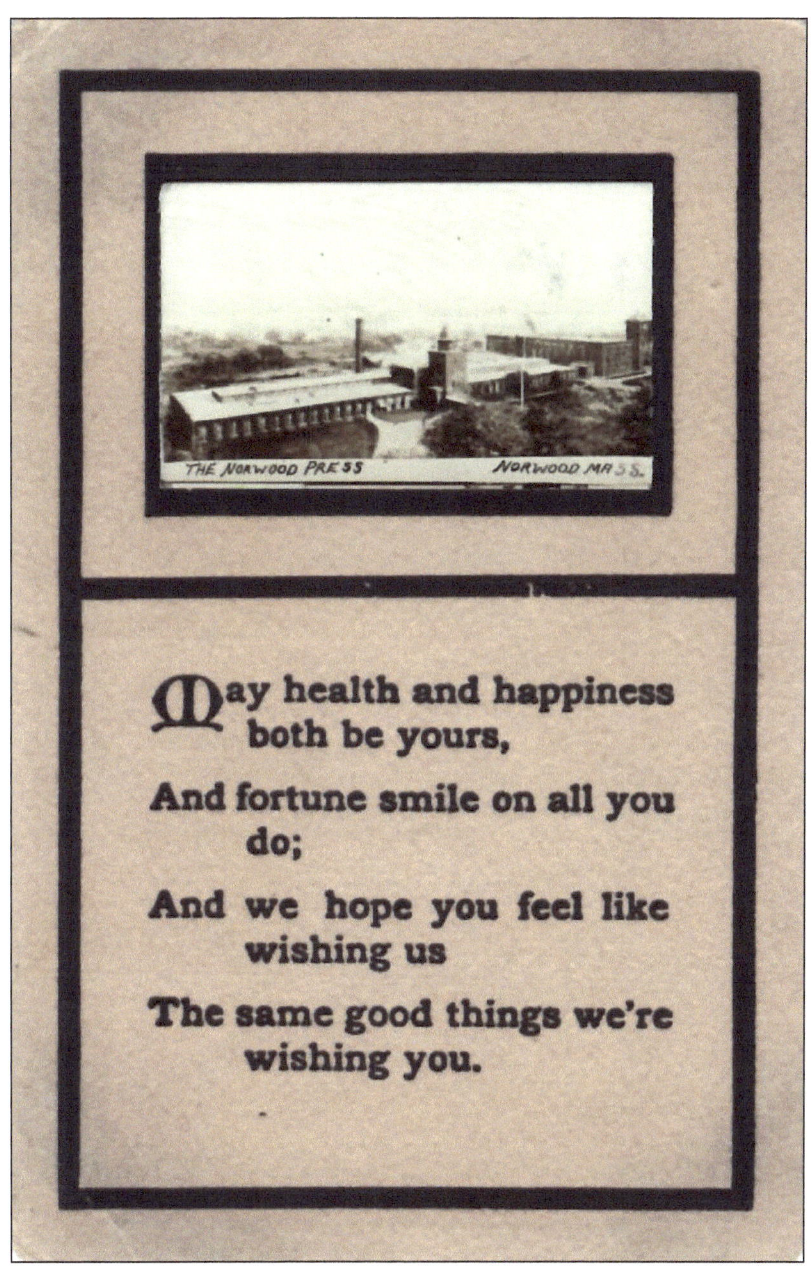

A variety of messages – some humorous, some inspirational – were printed on the stock postcards published by the Quality Photo Postal Company of St. Paul, Minnesota. Communities, businesses, or organizations could personalize them by adding an image. Here, a photograph of the Norwood Press was tipped onto a card which wishes health and happiness to all.

BIBLIOGRAPHY & FURTHER READING

Everett, Win. *Remembering Norwood: Win Everett's Tales of Tyot*, edited by Heather S. Cole and Edward J. Sweeney (Charleston, SC: The History Press, 2008).

Fanning, Patricia J. *Influenza and Inequality: One Town's Tragic Response to the Great Epidemic of 1918* (Amherst, MA: University of Massachusetts Press, 2010).

Fanning, Patricia J. *Keeping the Past: Norwood at 150* (Staunton, VA: American History Press, 2021).

Fanning, Patricia J. *Norwood: A History* (Charleston, SC: Arcadia Publishing, 2002).

Grove, John M. *Images of America: Norwood* (Charleston, SC: Arcadia Publishing, 1997).

Tinker, Francis. "History of Norwood, Massachusetts," *History and Directory of Norwood, Massachusetts for 1890* (Boston: Press of Brown Bros., 1890).

Tolles, Bryant Franklin, Jr. *Norwood: The Centennial History of a Massachusetts Town* (Norwood, MA: Town of Norwood, 1973).

ABOUT THE AUTHOR

Patricia J. Fanning is a life-long resident of Norwood, Massachusetts and professor emerita of sociology at Bridgewater State University. A former president of the Norwood Historical Society and current president of the Old Parish Preservation Volunteers, she has written several books related to the town of Norwood including *Norwood: A History* (2002), *Images of America: South Norwood* (2004), *Influenza and Inequality: One Town's Tragic Response to the Great Epidemic of 1918* (2010), *Keeping the Past: Norwood at 150* (2021), and *Old Parish Cemetery of Norwood, Massachusetts* (2023).